WIMBLEDON
The Hidden Drama

OTHER BOOKS BY GWEN ROBYNS

Vivien Leigh: Light of a Star
Royal Ladies
Royal Sporting Lives
Margaret Rutherford

WIMBLEDON
The Hidden Drama

GWEN ROBYNS

DAVID & CHARLES
NEWTON ABBOT

0 7153 6062 0

Set in 12 pt Centaur 1 pt leaded
and printed in Great Britain
by Latimer Trend & Company Ltd Plymouth
for David & Charles (Holdings) Limited
South Devon House   Newton Abbot   Devon

Contents

List of Illustrations

To
Jill Cohen, whose idea it was,
and
all my friends at the All England
Lawn Tennis and Croquet Club

CHAPTER 1

The Magic of Wimbledon

The All England Lawn Tennis and Croquet Club's Championship at Wimbledon is the greatest tennis show on earth.

It is an anachronism that I hope will go on as long as the grass grows green. It is a bland mixture of English garden party atmosphere with hard-core professional organisation. It is an emotional encounter between the great tennis players of the world and a most sophisticated, discerning public. It is a fortnight of beauty, nervous tension, professional vendettas, courage and the opportunity of seeing the human body perform miracles of grace and strength.

Forget all the talk about the brilliance of play on clay or the supremacy of the new synthetic courts. Dwell on the magic when a small white ball skims the world's most cherished square of grass. It is the end of a symphony, the climax of a ballet.

Feel the impact of that great Centre Court as it heaves, sweats and suffers with each final match. Note the ordinary man and woman watching become superior beings as they 'will' the underdog to victory. The Wimbledon crowds have always been partisan to the unexpected or the young player.

This is a tradition and splendour that men and women are prepared to travel the world to see. That has inspired in every school child who holds a racket a dream to some day go to Wimbledon. Enjoy for a while the glory and the grandeur of this event that remains steadfast in a world where commerce and psychological brainwashing are taking over the sports scene.

All this is due to a small group of men who make up the working committee of the All England Lawn Tennis and Croquet Club. Seen round a committee table, they look as if they could have been culled from any lunchtime gathering in a London club—gentle in demeanour, courteous in manner, deceptively mild and brilliantly tough.

The All England Lawn Tennis and Croquet Club is unique in every aspect. It is among the most selective and exclusive in the world. There are exactly 325 male members and 75 women, excluding the champions who become honorary members. Each year 90 temporary members are elected on a yearly basis.

For fifty weeks of the year they live in recluse splendour. Behind closed doors they are working and planning to make their club as efficient and beautiful as humanly possible. And then for one glorious period affectionately called 'The Fortnight', they permit the public to join them. In return they demand and expect good behaviour, strict obedience to the Wimbledon code and sportsmanship par excellence. And that is what it is all about.

The setting is so traditional and spiritual that you catch your breath. Down Church Road hill leaving the old Wimbledon Village behind you, past the expensive flats and St Mary's Church on the right and there lying at the bottom is the Wimbledon fantasy—the All England Lawn Tennis and Croquet Club.

The Centre Court, dominating the forty acres, is not beautiful by architectural standards. It is too bulky, too overbearing. It has the brutal quality of the experimental architecture of fifty years ago. But time, and the gentleness of its virginia creeper overlay, have softened the façade until it looks like a noble dowager who wears her jewels with panache.

Wimbledon is more than tennis. It is a complex composed of 15 grass courts, 10 hard ones (2 of which are covered), a bank, police station, post office, wine cellar and 15 restaurants that only open during 'The Fortnight'. It is also an undefinable spirit.

It is 9am on the opening day of Wimbledon. It could be any year, so little changes. I feel a heel showing my pass at the great wrought-iron gates in front of the queue that formed in the early hours of the morning. They are cheerful and lively and ready for brisk back-chat. The uniformed attendants do not recognise my face and are suspicious, checking me twice.

Because this is Wimbledon there is an air of restraint. No hysteria, no panic. For eleven and a half months a trained staff of experts have worked for this day.

I chat to the gardener heeling in the last of the plants. Fifteen years ago Woodward of Cheam was just a small nursery but along with Wimbledon they have grown until now this is their biggest contract. Every year 1,500 hydrangeas, 1,000 geraniums, 3,600 antirrhinums, 1,000 petunias, 500 French marigolds and 36 abulion lilies have to be planted. Watering begins at 5.30 every morning and continues from mobile watering cans that push their way through the crowds during the day. Climbing roses tumble on distant walls and trellises, and plumb in the centre of the grounds is a small Grimm's fairy-tale cottage with an apron garden dizzy with roses. Robert Twynam, the head groundsman, and his wife live there.

'It's everything I dreamed of,' says a nurse from New Zealand, who clocks in as a waitress.

'I haven't missed a year since 1946,' says the hefty man from Boston ahead in the queue.

It is so unruffled and orderly one wonders why. David Mills (ex-major 9th Gurkhas) walks around behind the dark glasses that he will wear for the next fortnight. He hopefully thinks that they will bring him anonymity. The gates swing open as the Lyons' navy vans with yellow lettering make their last minute 'fragile goods' deliveries. The bulk of the food is delivered before 9am.

The programme-sellers move into their small booths. They are a smart lot with well-set hair, trim blue pinafore dresses and white polo-necked sweaters. They smell of hair spray and English toilet water.

I run into Bob Twynam on the Grand Walk, a tough little

man who wears his pale blue Shetland polo-necked sweater like a native. His lean face is craggy and sun-tanned, topped with a mass of wavy grey hair. His manner is brisk and authoritative. This is not the time for idle talk.

'She's coming along nicely. We just need a bit of sunshine to top her off.' He speaks of his Centre Court which he has worked on for the last 345 days to bring to perfection this day, this hour.

Everywhere one sees groups of young men laughing, chatting. These are the students who year after year volunteer to clean the entire grounds. Later I talk to their leader Dr Philip Grover, but now I am too shy and just nod and pass on.

At the bookstall Elsie and George Allen are putting out their final postcards. For a number of years they have operated the bookstall which sells tennis books and postcards. It is an amusing fortnight for them in their otherwise razzmatazz Fleet Street lives.

It is 11am and the covers are taken off the self-service bonbon stands. This idea was introduced to Wimbledon from Switzerland in 1955. The students behind the counters begin filling each bin to overflow. The effect is magical—Aladdin's cave in sugar as the forty varieties shine like cabochon jewels. Solemnly they dust them with all the care of vendeuses at Cartiers. The mints sparkle like emeralds as the morning sun seeps through. Over one and a half million boiled sweets will be eaten during 'The Fortnight'.

The verandah of the Members' Stand, with its great crest and swag of purple and green, the Wimbledon colours, is ablaze with hydrangeas and trailing pink geraniums. There is a curtain of water drops as the window-boxes are sprinkled for the last time today.

The student cleaners, a motley crew in today's anything-goes-clothes, vanish in thin air to man the court covers in case of rain. The chairman, Herman David, pokes his head out from a window. His days will be filled with minor irritants but at this moment there is nothing more he can do. He wears the preoccupied air of a general before battle commences.

It is midday: the gates are opened. The rush begins. In from the north and south entrances comes the noise of people running.

Down they sweep, the hundreds of people who have been queueing for standing room on the Centre Court. Each man for himself as they charge with stools and sleeping blankets, baskets, umbrellas and plastic bags.

There is nothing sour or tired about them. They are laughing and shouting as hair flying they rush up the wide staircase to the Centre Court. For them 'The Fortnight' has really begun. What does it matter if they have to stand another eight hours? They are now within the enclave and savouring the magic of Wimbledon.

The first of the players begin to arrive as a motor cavalcade of dazzling white cars, each flying the Wimbledon pennant, sweeps through the gates. In previous years, it was sombre black Rolls-Royces, Daimlers and Austin Princesses. Last year British Leyland offered to do the job free with Morris Marinas and super 'dolly' drivers in white shirts, periwinkle blue minis and matching forage caps. This saved the All England Club £15,000.

What was lost in tradition was gained in sparkle. In the days to follow we learned that some of the women players preferred the old style cars but from the men players it was a different story. The cars glide to a halt outside the main office. Everyone is smiling. This is a fiesta as the fans cluster round to see new faces, old favourites.

It is a luxurious gesture to lay on transport but like everything at Wimbledon there is a core of hard-headed common sense. It is a guarantee that players arrive on time and are not lost in the great maze of London. Each day they are picked up from their hotels, flats or lodging houses and taken home again. But it is more than practical. It turns ordinary tennis players who gather from all over the world for 'The Fortnight' into golden gods and goddesses who now behave like the stars they are.

At 1pm miraculously the restaurants begin filling up. The first customer sinks his teeth into the onion layer of a Wimpy. The gin and tonics begin to flow but the tray of Pimm's as yet remains undisturbed, waiting for daughters to arrive.

The Members' Enclosure takes on the lively air of a cocktail party as old friends embrace. The talk is eclectic—infectious.

'No, darling, they are not back from Bermuda yet; it was a wonderful wedding—I do like a good English wedding cake; just can't hear a word you are saying, old boy, my ears are bunged up; all the roses have black spot or greenfly or some wretched thing; they say Smith will win but I've got my own little bet on that Rumanian chap; Uncle George is joining us, it's his sixtieth Wimbledon; God, I feel old, is that really Borotra over there?; of course we'll all have strawberries; Susan had a hysterectomy and Arthur's got boils; can you imagine anyone admitting to being a Liberal; my dear, her husband left her nothing . . .'

It's 2pm. Like phantoms they have slid into their seats on the Centre Court. 'Iced lollies, iced lollies like John Newcombe has,' calls the cheeky vendor.

The officials check the net, the umpire walks measuredly across and climbs the ladder into his chair. The ball boys, scrubbed and smart in their purple and green All England sports shirts, kneel down ready at the side of the court. Stan Smith, the American army sergeant and the bookmakers' favourite for the championship, examines his racket in a nervous gesture. Hans Joachin, the merchant from Berlin, glances up at the arena.

One two, three seconds. The chattering subsides. A cathedral-like hush descends on the Centre Court.

'Play,' the umpire calls.

Another Wimbledon is under way.

CHAPTER 2

Birth of the All England Club

T he train from London whizzed by just as it rattled along in 1877 flanking the grounds at Worple Road where the All England Lawn Tennis and Croquet Club began.

For this is where it all started and the story of lawn tennis in England began. The grounds now belong to the Wimbledon Girls' High School and I had gone there to recapture the past. It was a muggy summer's day. Toni Roethling, thirteen-year-old daughter of the groundsman, bobbed along in front of me, her corn-coloured pony tail burning in the sun.

'There is the Centre Court, the hard one in the middle. That's where Suzanne Lenglen and those other ladies played.' The school had wanted the girls to play on both hard and grass courts, and oddly enough had chosen the historic centre one to be made into a hard court.

The club-house is a low brick villa with French doors and deep windows, the kind of house you would expect to find in an Oscar Wilde theatre set. Bees buzz round the honeysuckle rampaging the walls. Bushes of gaudy pink hydrangeas add blotches of colour in the July sun. This club-house built for £450 and set in four acres of fields was the first home of the All England Club.

Downstairs, where once tea was served to the players in their swirling skirts and knickerbocker suits, the girls now stack their lacrosse sticks against the walls. The floors were shiny and bare, and the room was empty except for the odd brown painted table and stick back chair. We went up the dingy brown staircase, the same one used by those early champions—Maud Watson, May Sutton Bundy, Mrs Hillyard, Elizabeth Ryan, Suzanne Lenglen.

'Here are the willow pattern basins,' Toni cried. 'Look, they must have been seconds. The pattern is blurred and they don't seem to meet properly.'

There were four large wash-basins, on the right set in the original marble slab. On the left, white painted wood formed the surround replacing the marble which must have cracked some years back. Gone, too, were the matching lavatories which had now been replaced with more mundane plumbing.

We looked across the courts from the upstairs windows. I was peopling them with busty ladies in wasp waists, picture hats, swirling barathea skirts, parasols and dashing gentlemen with handlebar moustaches, stove-pipe trousers and roving eyes.

I saw ghosts flitting the courts because in the mind's eye the giants of the tennis world are always present. It is that kind of game.

The courts looked small and peaceful in that special kind of English scene. Through the country lanes of England today in forgotten villages, one catches similar glimpses of rural grace. It was here that the All England Club became a reality that was to set a standard for lawn tennis that has never been surpassed in the world, that sealed the tone and tradition of the £10,000,000 Wimbledon tennis complex that we know today.

At first it was only croquet that was played on these Worple Road courts but the All England Croquet Club, as it was then called, discovered after a precarious life of seven years that croquet had its limitations. The club exchequer was almost empty.

Among its members were four gentlemen who, not content with croquet, preferred to hit a moving ball through the air with a racket. Not only did they add 'lawn tennis' to the name of the club but created the first lawn tennis championships a few months later.

Three of them—Julian Marshall, Henry Jones and C. G. Heath-cote, a stipendiary magistrate from Brighton—formed a sub-committee and framed not only the rules of the championships but virtually the rules of the game we know today. The fourth was J. H. Walsh, the editor of *The Field* in whose mahogany and leather office at 346 Strand, the All England Club was founded.

The game had originally arrived in England from France. The first recorded championships took place in Paris in 1427 and the winner was a woman called Margot of whom it was chronicled:

'She played her backhand very powerfully, very cunningly and very cleverly.'

The name had stemmed from the French word *tenir*—to hold, stay, cling on to, and there were many variations. It was called tenes, tennys, tennise, tennis or tenys. It was the call from the server as he was about to send the ball flying. The game was already known over much of the Continent and when the French knights took it to Florence in 1325 it was an immediate success among the flamboyant Florentines.

By the end of the sixteenth century Paris had 1,800 courts for a population of only a quarter of a million. They called it *jeu de paume*, game of the palm of the hand.

Once the game has crossed the Channel it was taken up by the aristocrats. Henry VIII in his prime used to play at Hampton Court, and Charles I liked a game before breakfast.

Tennis, as we know it today, dates back to the peculiar eccentri-city of forty-year-old Major Walter Clopton Wingfield (retired), a dandy with a goatee beard, black coat trimmed with Persian lamb and top hat. In his spare time he created puzzle games and minor inventions which he put on to the market.

With that peculiar ingenuity of the British he took the game of *jeu de paume*, inspired it with some of his own fantasy and came up with a version he called 'Sphairistike' after the Greek word for sphere and stick.

He shaped the court like an hour glass and the players were called 'hand-in' and 'hand-out'. 'Hand-in' alone could serve or score and on losing a stroke he became 'hand-out'.

The kit Major Wingfield designed was cumbersome compared with the balls and rackets used at Wimbledon today. For the cost of six guineas, the package included two pear-shaped tennis rackets, one net, twelve 'rubber cored and flannel covered' balls and a book of rules.

The game was 15-up, as in rackets, but instead of being set at 40-all the score was to be called deuce, then advantage as in the French game of tennis. *The Oxford Dictionary* defines 'deuce' as 'the state of score (40-all, games all) at which either party must gain two consecutive points or games to win'.

To be accurate, tennis had already been played in one form at the Edgbaston Cricket Club in Birmingham and several other clubs scattered round the country had already taken it up in a dilettante way. But it was Major Wingfield who went out for himself to get the game popularised. By calling it a Greek word he hoped to give it more cache among the wealthy middle class whom he wanted to buy his game to play in their country houses.

So this was where it all began. In the cupboards at Worple Road, Toni showed me copies of old engravings. All the original giants—Smith and Riseley, the Rev J. T. Hartley (1879 and 1880), C. W. Grinstant, H. F. Lawford, the Irish champion and winner of Wimbledon Gold Prize in 1884, E. Renshaw (1882 and 1883).

The family saw me off. Walter Roethling came to England as a prisoner of war and remained on, first pig farming, then landscape gardening and finally his present job as groundsman for these courts.

'It's been a bad year,' he explained. 'Too much wind has dried the grass.'

The 4.35 from Waterloo rattled by.

By 1880 tennis at Wimbledon was an established success. A lease for a further twelve years at Worple Road had been granted and additional dressing rooms had been installed by renting part of the premises at the rear of the pavilion. At the end of the financial year there was a profit of £230 as compared with 1s 10d in 1879. There were two movable grandstands now and ball boys were provided by the club on Saturdays. The charge of admission was raised from 1s to 2s 6d and the attendance was declared 'to rival that at Lord's last week in beauty and fashion'. It was also the year of the first scoreboard, this being a necessity due to the noise of the passing trains drowning the umpire's voice. Technicalities in the game itself were changed with the net lowered at the posts from 5ft to 4ft.

This year with its three innovations—lowered net, the placing of both feet of the server behind the baseline and the fact that players now changed sides after every odd game—laid down the principles of lawn tennis as we know it today throughout the world.

It was into this world that the two Renshaw brothers of Cheltenham appeared. These twins of nineteen years of age had won the doubles championship at Oxford and had stunned onlookers with the brilliance of what was to become known as 'the Renshaw smash'.

The brothers with their neat moustaches were dashingly handsome, although there was nothing in their slender physiques to disclose their fantastic power. William had already shown his mettle when he won the Irish championship.

In his scholarly book *Wonderful Wimbledon* (Pelham Books) Alastair Revie describes the brothers.

'Both twins were powerfully built young men whose stamina was greater than that of most opponents they encountered. They were also accomplished strategists and good stroke players. Willie possessed one of the earliest power-play services of the game and could also take the ball early with his ground strokes instead of on the drop. He was first rate at the net and was sound overhead. Ernest was a more delicate and sensitive player, possessing most of the strokes and using them with a smoother and more graceful style. Both were capable, when the occasion demanded, of developing all-court volleying attacks.'

They were also typical of the amateurs who were now taking up tennis seriously, and form the foundation pattern of the club membership as we know it today.

CHAPTER 3

The First Family of Wimbledon

I f there ever was a first family of Wimbledon it is the Sterry-Cooper alliance. Since the early days of 1894 there has always been a Sterry or Cooper in the All England Club. They are as ubiquitous as strawberries and cream.

What the Renshaws did for men's tennis, the Sterrys and Coopers did for the women. There was the original Charlotte Cooper (Mrs Alfred Sterry), champion of the nineties. Her daughter Gwen (Mrs Max Simmers) and niece Valerie (Mrs Peter Weatherall) are still members.

I was sitting in the Members' Enclosure with Tony Cooper, now assistant secretary of the club by way of stockbroking in the City. He and his cousin, Rex Sterry (a committee member), are the last remaining males in a family whose very existence is woven in the tapestry of Wimbledon. They are both endearing characters, the one like Stilton and the other mellow as Gorgonzola.

'Ah yes, Aunt "Chatty",' Tony Cooper said. 'Of course I remember as a child being taken by her to Worple Road.

'Extraordinary, isn't it. You know she was in the days of May Sutton, Lottie Dod and that incredible Irish champion, Maud Watson. Aunt "Chatty" first won the championship in 1894, then five times in all, and I think I'm right in saying that she never heard the ball bounce because she was stone deaf. She was very accurate, of course, and she always knew exactly what the score was. In 1908, at the age of thirty-seven, which was getting on in those days, she was the oldest woman ever to win Wimbledon. That year she won all three events.

'Aunt "Chatty" used to live with her parents in a red-brick wistaria-covered house called "Founhope" in Ewell Road, Surbiton. In fact, it was right next door to the house where I was born. One day in 1908 my father, Harry Cooper, was in the garden with a chum of his, pruning the roses or wistaria or something, when "Chatty" arrived on her bicycle. He called out to her, because everyone was fond of "Chatty". She was that sort of girl.

' "Where have you been, 'Chatty'?"

'Propping up her bicycle, she replied: "As a matter of fact I have been to Wimbledon and I've just won the championship."

' "Oh, have you," replied my father, and went on with his pruning.

'It was all taken rather for granted in those days. My aunt was, in fact, a jolly good player and even if she did wear a huge skirt almost to the ground and black shoes and stockings, she never served underarm and always used to rush up to the net. I remember that she cinched in her waist with a wide belt, the sort boys wear, with two silver buckles.'

Whatever Wimbledon meant to Charlotte Sterry, as she became on marriage, she was not overwhelmed by its splendour. After she died, the gold medal that she received as Britain's first Olympic tennis winner could not be found. Nor her Wimbledon trophies.

'Typical,' says Tony Cooper.

'I bet she gave it to the gardener,' says her son, Rex Sterry.

The Sterrys and the Coopers were closely intermarried, and Tony Cooper tried to unravel it for me.

'Well, you see Rex's old mum (Charlotte Sterry and née Cooper) is a sister of my father's and a first cousin of my mother's.'

After she married 'Aunt "Chatty" ' carried on the tradition for tennis by laying a court at her home called Braemar Lodge. It was, in fact, laid the wrong way but this was no obstacle for 'Chatty' Sterry, who was never one to be put off. She had it moved round the right way.

In the same year that Charlotte Cooper made her Wimbledon début, another Charlotte was making tennis history. This was the incredible Lottie Dod who became the youngest Wimbledon champion in history. She was only fifteen and played her way to match point with a man-size volley and overhead smash. Her forehand drive had the pace of a man's and defeated the holder in the challenge round with the loss of only two games.

Lottie would have made fashion headlines today. A sturdy little thing, like many of the other women she wore black shoes and stockings but her dress was considered very *avant garde*. Her favourite was an ankle length pleated skirt with a polo-necked over-dress cunningly looped up at one side. She pinned a sprig of white heather on the bodice for luck. Her hair was stuffed up under a white cap with only the fringe showing. Most of her friends wore nifty boater hats but Lottie stuck to her cap much as Helen Wills Moody made the eye-shade her own personal signature.

Like many of those early Wimbledon women players, Lottie came from the provinces. Cheshire, Worcestershire, Lancashire and the Midlands all produced good players simply because most private houses had tennis courts, and competition was strong. More affluent families even had two grass courts which were always immaculately kept. The standard of play was higher than home tennis today and most houses had tennis parties on Wednesday and Saturday afternoons.

In the mornings, the whole family were made to work, cutting, rolling and marking the court. The fish netting which was taken down at the end of the day had to be put up on iron posts—a beastly job. Balls were usually rubbed clean on the door mat.

By 3pm everyone had arrived on bicycles or in pony traps. The eldest brother usually arranged the order of play beginning with a spirited men's doubles. At 4.30 there was tea set in the dining-room. Home-made scones, strawberry, raspberry, gooseberry or black-currant jam. A bowl had been delivered to the milkman the night before for the Cornish cream to eat with the scones. There was a large jam sponge, sometimes with icing sugar on top, ginger, madeira and fruit cake. The mother in the family always presided over the water urn at the top of the table and the large dark brown teapot kept specially for tennis days. Everyone drank lashings of tea and talked of nothing but tennis and the forthcoming county championship. They were not pat-ball parties. Tennis was a serious matter. And at the end of the day, fortified by home-made lemonade for the girls and beer for the boys, everyone went home.

Lottie Dod was undoubtedly the Billie Jean King of her generation. She had a special kind of independent thinking and played to win. With the softer balls of those days and the slacker strung rackets the player required to have a great deal of accuracy and strength if she was to reach Lottie's standard. She had, in fact, as much versatility and more vigour than Suzanne Lenglen when the French wonder was of a corresponding age. The crowds used to call 'Lottie, Lottie,' as she foxed her opponent with her quick-witted shots.

Paradoxically, although Miss Dod had a powerful smash, she served underarm. She thought overarm placed too great a strain on women players! For six years she remained champion of the women players and then at her height and only twenty-one years old, she became bored with tennis and left to take up other interests.

Some time in the latter part of the fifties I remember in the swirling Wimbledon crowds at Earl's Court station, seeing a little old lady clutching a basket of raspberries. Her eyes were still bright despite her eighty-odd years and she appeared to be hurrying home. This was, in fact, Miss Lottie Dod who for the first time was too ill to go to Wimbledon, and followed it all that year on her radio.

Lottie Dod is perhaps the greatest all-round sportswoman that England has produced. She became an international hockey player, won the Women's Golf Championship and was second in the archery event in the Olympic Games in 1908. In addition, she was an expert horsewoman, skater, sculler and mountaineer. She died in 1960 at the age of eighty-eight years.

The ladies' championship at Wimbledon began in 1883 when

Miss Maud Watson won playing in a boater and elegant white dress. Another early woman player who influenced the future of tennis was Miss Blanche Bingley, who gained her tennis immortality only after she became Mrs G. W. Hillyard playing under her husband's initials. She became lady champion six times in all. Her championship tennis career spanned twenty-eight years and the fourteen years' gap between her first and last winning of the championship remains the record. On her silver wedding anniversary, she surprised everyone by playing a spirited game and reaching the singles semi-final.

Another of the 'greats' in those early days was Miss Dorothea Douglas who on marriage played as Mrs Lambert Chambers. From 1903 to 1914 she held the championship. During World War I she kept up her tennis and made a spectacular recovery in 1919 when she was twice within match point to the dashing young French girl Suzanne Lenglen before finally losing. Like many other women players she had graduated to tennis from badminton. A tactician of high calibre she was yet another woman player who proved that the real champion is a heady mixture of philosophy, strategy and stamina. She died in London in 1960, aged eighty-two and was a regular over the years holding an awed court in the Members' Enclosure.

The first American girl to play at Wimbledon was Miss May Sutton. With her Gibson girl figure and hair style, she appeared on the court wearing her skirts just above ankle length and sleeves to the elbow showing a fine stretch of arm. One of the English women players was so horrified that she made Miss Sutton let down her skirt a shade before she was allowed to play on the Centre Court. At the time she was only eighteen years old but it was her topped forehand drive of menacing strength that brought her into championship class.

CHAPTER 4

The 'Bounding Basque'

H

e was sitting in the far corner of the Members' Enclosure. A thin, well-preserved man with a finely bridged nose, well-manicured hands and nervous mannerisms like a bird. His suit was neat, dark and of continental cut. His eyes kept roving the scene as if looking for someone. It was a distinctive un-English face.

So this was Jean Borotra, the greatest of all showmen in the lawn tennis world. Today we have Nastase, Gonzales, Pilic, but none of them can match Borotra. As the 'Bounding Basque' he captivated Wimbledon with his charm, brilliance of play and wild, wild enthusiasm.

I had asked Dan Maskell, former Wimbledon professional, who had played so many times with him thirty to forty years ago, to brief me on the 'Bounding Basque'.

'The great thing was to walk on to the court with him. He really stirred the adrenalin in one he was so enthusiastic. People used to say, "Give me one more tennis player to watch in my life and it would be Borotra."

'Whether it was natural entertaining I still don't know or whether it was part of a private plan. But the great thing is that he was a man of tremendous vitality and this oozed out of him so that you were immediately involved in his personality. But beneath this veneer, if you could call it that, he had an ice-cold brain and he could look at everything in the most analytical term.

His whole game was based on what he was capable of doing and what the other man was. There was never a man like him to go into a match without having first summed up his opponent.'

There he sat. As I approached he got up to greet me and the vividness of this man of seventy-two summers was remarkable. He kissed my hand and I knew at once what this chemistry was that had sent women almost swooning off the court. He has 'charisma'.

Borotra first came to Wimbledon in 1922 when a new quartet of attractive personalities was seen together for the first time. They were immediately nicknamed the 'Four Musketeers'. This great team of Frenchmen—Brugnon, Borotra, Cochet and Lacoste —brought glory to France throughout the world in the years ahead.

Jacques ('Toto') Brugnon was the quiet, sensitive one who in doubles was willing to sublimate his own personality on the court and allow his partner to shine. He was a superb doubles player although he always preferred to play in the right court as he said he had no backhand. His strokes were reliable, well placed and directed with fiery accuracy. He and Borotra had both played at Worple Road where Brugnon's peculiar forehand 'slap' had caught everyone's eye.

Henri Cochet had once been a ball boy and grew up in the world of tennis. He could demoralise the hardest hitter by standing right inside the court and taking all the speediest shots on the rise. He had no service to speak of and no backhand, yet for five years running he ranked as the foremost player in the world. He was hair-raising in his ability to return the most awkward shots, and gave his fans a sense of invulnerability, a feeling of assured victory simply because he himself believed that nothing was impossible.

Cochet was the kind of good-humoured player that Wimbledon enjoyed. He was human. There were days he played like a genius and others he seemed to fold up, much as Evonne Goolagong has her walk-about days. When he was put out of the tournament in only the second round in 1932 by a Scottish doubles player I. G.

Collins, he immediately entered for the All England Plate open to anyone who had had the misfortune to be knocked out in the first or second round. Up till then no important player had thought it prudent to do this, but by doing so, and incidentally winning it, Cochet gave it status and encouraged many others to do the same.

René Lacoste was a fantastic example to youth as he had no special talent except his gift of physique. Son of a great industrialist he persuaded his father to allow him to interrupt his studies to try and become a tennis champion and help France by playing in the Davis Cup. He worked six hours a day, made a note of all the great matches he saw, kept a diary on why every player won or lost a match, read all the books on tennis he could find and yet had still to see that he never became stale. It was sheer guts that brought him up to championship class. He could have been the greatest of the four, but by the time he was twenty-four he had burned himself out and had to retire through ill health.

London society and tennis hostesses scratched each others' eyes out to capture the foursome. The great country homes were opened to them. They were the darlings of the Savoy cocktail bar.

'Tell me how did it all begin, M Borotra?' I asked.

'I would perhaps never have played tennis if my mother, a widow with four young children of whom I was the eldest, had not realised as early as the beginning of the century the importance of learning languages. She sent me to England in the summer of 1912 when I was a boy of twelve to polish my English. The arrangement was that I would spend two months with the Wildy family at Shord Hill and their son went to our home near Biarritz.

'There was a tennis court at Shord Hill and I had been asked, of course, if I played tennis which I did not. So, at any of the garden parties I was asked to play croquet, billiards or bridge, but never tennis. One day Mrs Wildy told me: "Jean, I looked at you yesterday when you were watching tennis and you can't tell me that you are not longing to try."

'I could not deny it. So she went for her rackets, put one in my hand and asked me: "Jean, do you think you could send the ball back over the net if I sent it towards you from the other side, or would you miss it?''

'She did not know that I could have sent it back with the palm of my hand, right or left, as I had done that for years against a pelota wall in my village. We went on the court and she was so surprised when the ball came back and back again, shot after shot. The next day we had a game and she told the whole village of Kenley about a young Basque who had never played tennis and still was able to take part in a game. From then on I played every day and loved it.

'Then the war came, when I was lieutenant in the army. After 1918, studies again for the tough entrance competition at École Polytechnique. It was only when I spent my holidays in Biarritz that I played at all. My brother Fred, four years younger than I, in the last two years had become the best player in Biarritz. At the end of the summer playing with him, I won the Biarritz Tournament thanks to the athletic and volleying game and the quick reflexes developed by the game of pelota. My opponent in the final was so surprised that he convinced me to enter the Racing Club de France, my first club, of which I am still a member. Over the next two years I managed to play three or four times a week on covered wood courts and in the winter of 1922 I won the French National Championship. So that is how I became to be sent to Wimbledon that year with Lacoste, Cochet and Brugnon. Alas, we each lost to one member of the Australian team.'

Borotra became one of the world's greatest volleyers of all time, in spite of the fact that he used to change his grip from backhand to forehand which so many people criticise these days.

'I suppose that I learnt as much from Borotra as anybody when I was younger at Wimbledon,' Dan Maskell told me. 'He was a great flatterer as he used to say to me: "Whenever I come to play you are getting better and better. I see you a tremendous player of the future." To a young man this is heady stuff.

'Perhaps the thing that is interesting is that when he was in his middle forties playing in the singles at Wimbledon and I was playing with him one day, he was doing these ra-ta-ta-ta volleys quickly at the net in a highly competitive sort of way. The first time in my life I saw him mistime a volley, not because he had misjudged the ball but because he was slow, just a fraction slow, in changing his grip from forehand to backhand. It was a technical sort of thing but I immediately recorded it mentally. I mentioned this, which was perhaps a bit cruel, and said:

' "Jean, in all our years of practising together this is the first time I saw you not get your grip in time." He blushed slightly and replied: "Oh no, no, Dan." I said: "Oh yes, those things don't fool me. I have had too many years as a teacher to miss that."

'Quarter of an hour later he hit another and I thought this really would be rubbing it in to mention it again, but he knew that I knew and I knew that he knew and it was then—and remember he was forty—that it seemed to me that by his standards, he was slipping. But really it was remarkable that he still played so magnificently.

'In his heyday, Borotra was so fast that, like Stanley Matthews the footballer, he was so quick off the mark that in three or four yards he gathered such momentum that it could take him past where he had struck the ball. Time and time again he had to save himself by stepping up on to the barricade.'

There were times, too, when the 'Bounding Basque' did a quick flip into the lap of one of the public sitting in the front row. With panache he always raised his beret before hurrying on his way. That, in fact, he invariably chose the lap of a pretty girl and was so obligingly caught by the camera is another story.

Dan Maskell who as the former Wimbledon tennis coach knows more about these early 'greats' of tennis, told me of his most outstanding memory of Borotra.

'It was not at Wimbledon actually, but at Queen's Club. It was an international club match with Borotra playing Tilden, both at the height of their genius. They played on the east court, court number 1. The gallery was packed to suffocation. It was a fantastic match of speed . . . these two great men. The spell-binding thing was not only the tennis, but Borotra trying to get to the net and

Tilden trying to keep him back with disguised lobbing and so on. If one is aware of people and what makes them tick this was a fascinating study of two great personalities, great rivals, each fully understanding the other man's capabilities. In the end Borotra won after two long sets, I think.

'It always stands out to me that the drama of tennis is not in the technicalities of hitting a little white ball, but in the clash of personalities, the clash of rivalries and the international element. All these things that go to make a man give more than he is capable of giving whatever his ideal is: for his country or for his own personal glory. In many ways it is like being an actor.'

Every great player at Wimbledon has legends that are woven round his name. Some are true, others stuff that dreams are made of, while others can be frankly malicious gossip.

But Borotra's were always glamorous. They still talk at Wimbledon of how he used to literally drop in from the skies just before his matches, clutching an armful of roses for the girls in the office. He used an airplane as players use motor cars today. Transatlantic tennis is accepted today, but forty-six years ago trans-Channel smacked of real panache.

Borotra has always had to earn his own living and Wimbledon was shuffled in between business appointments round the world for the French petrol pump business with which he is still associated. As his main customers were the oil companies, whose headquarters were in the capital cities of the world, he always managed to fiddle his business trips to coincide with the various tennis tournaments. Quite often he would fly across from Paris on the Saturday night before Wimbledon, have a knock up and then attend the international dinner. Back to Paris Sunday morning, returning just in time to play on the Centre Court on Monday.

In 1926, year of the golden jubilee of the All England Club, was his closest shave in arriving on time. Thirty-three masters of tennis had been lined up for the arrival of King George V and Queen Mary, to whom they were to be presented. It was Wimbledon's finest hour. They stood there in a row, only one familiar sight was missing—the black beret of Jean Borotra. The nervous tension of the committee and the players relayed itself to the crowd. Suzanne Lenglen could scarcely keep her feet still as she hopped around like an excited child. Suddenly the 'Bounding Basque' bounced on to the court.

'Am I too late?' he asked. His plane had been delayed by fog and he had had to change into his tennis flannels in a car which was standing by waiting at the airport. Norah Gordon Cleather, the assistant secretary, grabbed his rackets from him as he stepped into place at the end of the line. The crowd adored his audacity.

Later in the day, after I had talked to Borotra, I wandered up to court number 11 to see him play in the veterans' match, partnered by R. Abdesselam against J. J. Fitzgibbon and R. J. McCabe of Ireland. Behind me was the roar of the Centre Court and the bustle of court number 1. Here there was just a sprinkling of spectators as four elderly gentlemen had the time of their lives. If their tummies were slightly rounder, their hair thinner, and the Basque bounding slower it did not matter. They had made Wimbledon for yet another year.

As Borotra summed up:

'The atmosphere of the place has remained much the same as when I first came. The singles championship is still what it was —the Blue Riband of lawn tennis, the winning of which is still the ambition of all the great players. With its organisation and its tradition of good manners and fair play, Wimbledon remains unique in the world. Some things have changed, of course, and one cannot deny that the lady players' clothes are more interesting than fifty years ago . . .'

CHAPTER 5

Suzanne In

T he charm of Wimbledon today is that the All England
Club is young enough and its members old enough that
comparisons with the early days are intriguing and in-
evitable. As long as Wimbledon is spoken about, Mlle Suzanne
Lenglen will be remembered, and every year as a bright crop of new
players come up they are invariably compared with her. And the
answer is still the same year after year:

'Suzanne would beat the lot.'

'Every time she played anybody, it was like a cat playing with
a mouse. She literally did what she liked with the ball,' Mrs
Forsland (Eileen Bennett) told me. 'What people don't understand today is that she could hit as hard as anybody but she
simply did not have to. She was a beautiful volleyer and had
magnificent overhead shots just as good as any of these girls here
today.'

We were sitting in the Members' Enclosure near the fountain
ringed with blue hydrangeas. We had just come from the Centre
Court where the reigning champion, Evonne Goolagong, had been
beaten by Billie Jean King from America. Invariably the comparisons began . . . and once more the whole mystique of Suzanne
Lenglen is re-told. She brought more publicity and world-wide
recognition to the game than anyone has ever done in the history
of lawn tennis.

It was in 1913 that the first rumours of a new star reached

34

Worple Road. People back from the South of France spoke in awe of a surprising fifteen-year-old girl who played tennis like a goddess tormented from the sidelines by her sagacious father.

They told how Papa Lenglen, a former cycling champion, trained his prodigy by scattering one franc pieces on the court which if she hit, she was allowed to spend. And when she tired of this, he scattered pieces of paper as small as snowflakes which the delighted girl had to hit and pin down.

All through the war years in the sun-baked courts of the South of France, he trained her relentlessly, far in excess of the conditioning given the young players today. Suzanne *had* to win. She never played for anything else. There was no 'gloire' in those days but just the 'déshonneur' whenever she lost a game.

Suzanne did not come to Worple Road until 1919, the year of the regeneration of the All England Lawn Tennis and Croquet Club after four debilitating war years. The public was hungry for a new idol and who better to fill it than this slender girl with her vociferous charm? For the real lovers of the game she brought a new kind of calculated expertise and for the dilettante a glorious grace and glamour that had not been seen at Wimbledon before. Until then there had been several competent women players but no one had the star quality of Suzanne, the first woman to combine the alchemy of show business and sport. She mesmerised the crowds. She bloomed under their affection. 'The bigger the crowd the better,' she would say in her French accent heavily overlaid with American.

Worple Road had a bonanza year in 1919 with its first royal cast which included George V, Queen Mary and the Princess Royal who were all paying their first visit. This was just the social fillip that the club needed and the crowds for the first time were queuing to sleep overnight just as they do today. It was into this frenetic atmosphere that the sallow-skinned girl with a beaky nose, the figure of a ballerina and the will power of a long-distance runner stepped.

She immediately electrified the crowds as she would do for the next six years. No other player at Wimbledon since has had the same following and the queues she brought year after year became known as 'Lenglen trails'.

Even Suzanne's tennis clothes were different, setting a pattern that was to be slavishly copied throughout the world. She threw away girdles and cumbersome petticoats and liberated the female figure.

For her début, she chose a simple short-sleeved, round neck dress with an accordian-pleated skirt, and a white piqué pull-on cloche that came down over her ears. She had not yet found the fashion sense which followed her in the coming years. The most one could say of her was that she looked 'different'.

Her championship match that year with Mrs Lambert Chambers is now tennis history. From the start Mrs Chambers, a sporting player if ever there was one, had everything loaded against her. She was the older woman by years, the reigning champion who had had to spend the last four years of the war 'out to grass'. In those days the champions did not compete in 'The Fortnight' as today; they sat on the sideline waiting for the eventful day when they would be challenged.

By the time the championship day came, the young and brilliant Suzanne had gained a psychological advantage simply because the crowds already adored her. Just as the two players were to begin play the rain poured down. The court was quickly covered and the two women banished to the poky dressing-rooms which were so unlike the lavish ones of today. The hours passed until late in the afternoon the game was called off. With hindsight it should have been an advantage to the older woman playing on her own home ground but it had the opposite effect. Next day when the match came to be played, she visibly showed the nervous tension she had been under during the last twenty-four hours. She had had a rough night and scarcely slept.

The first set was won by the spirited Suzanne 10–8, and the second one 6–4 to Mrs Chambers. When Suzanne's energy began to flag Papa Lenglen threw her sugar lumps spiked with brandy and shouted encouragement. The crowds wallowed in such high drama and Gallic extroversion.

In the third set with the crowds almost hysterical, Mrs Chambers reached 6–5 and 40–15. She later sportingly said that it was at this precise moment her mind began to speculate what the newspapers would say now as they had tipped Suzanne to win. Mrs Chambers finally lost the game 9–7. It was the kind of frenzied finale that the Wimbledon crowd loves.

At the end of the match both players were too mentally and physically exhausted to be presented to the King and Queen. Mrs Chambers made her dignified retreat and Suzanne was swept into the emotional embraces of her formidable parents. She had not let papa down and now at last the Lenglen fortunes were assured!

From then on the Lenglen success was confirmed. She went on to win the singles championship six times (and, in fact, was never beaten) and the doubles six times with her partner, American Elizabeth Ryan. Suzanne with her elegant ballerina body and movements, and Elizabeth Ryan, twelve-stone's worth of strength and might, complemented each other like oysters and stout. Suzanne had a long stride and stretched her arms often right across into her partner's court. This suited Miss Ryan who could get into stride with her famous chop, and bring the ball down to people's feet.

'I just loved standing there and killing that ball,' Miss Ryan says today. 'Whatever Suzanne was like off court, I always found her most professional and not at all temperamental when we played. We did not need to speak as we understood each other's game.'

By the time she returned to Wimbledon in 1920 as reigning champion, Suzanne Lenglen had become a transformed person. The *gauche* young woman had become a fascinating *belle laide* and capitalised on her newly acquired chic. Every Paris couturier wanted to dress her, but it was from Patou that she took her lead.

Few tennis players used make-up at all in those days, but Suzanne loaded her face with a heavy ochre to cover her bad skin and matched her lipstick to her bandeau, even if it was mauve. Off court she elongated her eyebrows with pencil until they turned up at the ends in a comical curl. The Centre Court crowds came as much to be shocked and exhilarated by this extraordinary Frenchwoman who stopped to make up her lips when changing ends and took a sip of champagne or brandy from a bottle she kept on the sidelines.

They loved that she dared to be different and even wore the first silk see-through dresses. Years later 'Gorgeous Gussy' Moran from America was to cause a sensation with her lacey panties, but it was nothing compared to the electric thrill that went through the crowds when they caught their first glimpse of Suzanne's bare leg above her stockings which she had rolled just above the knees. It was superb show business.

Even the way she posed for the cameras was different with her hand on one hip and bent knee like the fashionable Parisian mannequins, and no one dared question her taste when she walked to the Centre Court wearing a brown rabbit skin coat over her tennis dress. No tennis star today could match that for aplomb!

CHAPTER 6

Suzanne Out

T he first game Suzanne Lenglen ever lost at Wimbledon was to a young unknown player Elsie Goldsack (Lady Furlonge).

'I was in the rabbit warren (downstairs ladies' dressing-room) when the umpire came and knocked on the door.

' "Why aren't you coming? You have kept Suzanne waiting twenty minutes."

'I was petrified as he led me out to meet her. I remember it so well. She was wearing a mauve bandeau and had lips to match.

'The umpire then said:

' "Miss Goldsack is very nervous."

'Which, of course, made me fifty times worse. We didn't have a refrigerator for iced drinks in those days just two sorts of goldfish bowls. One was lemon and the other water.

' "What funny coloured water," I chirped up out of sheer nerves.

'We then started knocking up. Suzanne had already beaten two internationals 6-0, 6-0 and she was leading me in the end 5-0, but I was leading 40-30 when she put up a lob. I thought shall I shut my eyes and slam it, as I was playing very well for me. By the time I had made up my mind it was almost on my nose but I hit back and won the game.

'It was the first game Suzanne had ever lost at Wimbledon. People went mad and threw their hats in the air. She lost five games at Wimbledon in 'The Fortnight' and I had got one of them. She lost two to 'Bunny' Ryan in the semi-final and two to Joan Fry in the final.

'We never thought about going to bed early and training as they do today. During 'The Fortnight' I went to a cocktail party every night and had a little drink of champagne. The only thing that ever put me off was a smoke-filled room.

'There was also another difference. We always had a little chat as we changed ends and asked:

' "Who are you going out with tonight?"

'Tennis has lost its fun. We took our matches seriously but we had a much more human approach than today. And I don't think we were any the worse for it.'

The loss of this game, traumatic as it was, was nothing to the humiliation to come.

Suzanne Lenglen's fall from grace at Wimbledon arose from a confrontation between a strong-minded woman and the establishment side of the All England Lawn Tennis Club. The story is now forty-seven years old but it could in effect have taken place last year. I feel that the official attitude would have been the same. Whatever else happens in our permissive age, the standards of behaviour at Wimbledon remain the same. Whether it is over advertising on dresses, shouting at the linesmen or keeping royalty waiting, the club has its own hard and fast rules.

This, then, is the story of the fall of an idol and the sheer tragedy of it all. Had this not taken place perhaps Suzanne Lenglen would not have turned professional as soon as she did and terminated that brilliant international career while still in her thirties.

Teddy Tinling gives the background so vital to the finale of this tragedy.

'It is spring 1926 when Suzanne is having a fight with the French Lawn Tennis Federation because they want to break her unbeaten partnership with American Elizabeth Ryan and ask her to play with Didi Vlasto, a young French player. Suzanne already knows that Elizabeth Ryan, too, is half inclined to split up be-

cause she has been asked by the American authorities to partner
an American.

'Sitting on the fence there is also Helen Wills, a new threat
from America to her supremacy. Suzanne's future in her own
mind has now got to be confirmed. Weeks go by of mental anguish
and indecision, and she finally faces up to playing Helen Wills at
Cannes.'

This game was, in fact, one of the toughest Suzanne ever had
to play. From his sick-bed her father had warned her that it
would be no walkover. He also insisted that no American umpires
or linesmen officiated. Helen's friends counteracted by demanding
that no French officiate either. This, then, was the mood—
suspicious, aggressive, apprehensive.

On the day of the game a porridge-faced Suzanne set out to
defend her title. With her usual panache, her friend Lady Wavertree stood on the sideline with sips of champagne when she
changed ends. No orange cordial for Suzanne!

Suzanne won 6–3, 8–6, but that was not the kind of score that
she was used to. Surrounded by flowers she burst into tears as
her young American opponent left the court unnoticed.

For the moment the sun shone once more and Suzanne was
thinking of another Wimbledon. Everything was going to be fine
and she would play better tennis than ever before and the crowds
would once more call in adulation 'Suzanne, Suzanne'.

On arrival at Wimbledon one of the hazards that faced her was
the championship draw. In those days there was no seeding in the
doubles, and Suzanne was distinctly annoyed at the results. When
the draw was made there were forty-eight women's doubles pairs,
but in the first round destiny took its shape. She found herself up
against Elizabeth Ryan, her old partner of so many victories, and
Mary Browne, who had already tested her severely in the recent
Paris championship.

'How can they be so tactless?' she asked. 'I, Suzanne, who have
brought more money and more people to Wimbledon than anyone
else. How could they do this to me?'

It was into this turbulent set-up that Suzanne arrived at

Wimbledon. She was patently upset and everything seemed black.

In defending herself later, she always denied that she knew of a singles match which had been scheduled for 3pm, that the referee Mr Burrow had only told her of her important doubles to be played on the Centre Court at 4pm and nothing else. It had been the practice of the previous All England Club secretary, Commander Hillyard, to personally inform the pampered Suzanne of her programme for the following day. Mr Burrow had left her to find her schedule from the referee's office or the morning list in *The Times*, as all the other players did.

Here the stories differ. Norah Gordon Cleather, then the personal assistant to the secretary of the club, was under the impression that Suzanne did know of the two matches before leaving Wimbledon on the previous night and that she had said quite firmly that she would not play the single before the doubles, and left the referee's office to sort it out.

Borotra looking back today gallantly says:

'I am sure that she did not know that she was to play two matches. I think Brugnon did tell her at twelve o'clock. Suzanne was then going off to the doctor with her sore shoulder. She asked the operator in the small Victoria Hotel near Trafalgar Square where she was living—you see she had very little money then— to ring Mr Burrow and cancel the first match. But there were not enough lines perhaps and on that day everyone was trying to get through. The hotel may not have realised how important it was and not succeeding, gave up. But off she went. First to the doctor and then to lunch with her old friend, Lady Wavertree. What she should have done was to call a taxi and send word if she could not get through by 'phone. Had I been there I would have done this for her.'

Teddy Tinling says:

'Knowing her, I would think that she probably knew that the officials had contradicted her wishes and just thought: "I am Suzanne. What are they going to do about it?" '

Mrs Leslie Godfree (Kitty McKane, who had played her many

times) thinks on hindsight that Didi Vlasto rang her at midday to tell her and Suzanne had said: 'Oh, I can't possibly come. I have been to see my doctor and he says that one match is enough for me and now I am going out to lunch.'

Elizabeth Ryan says that she knows the truth, but even at this stage in her long life she is not telling!

'There were endless unnecessary misunderstandings,' says Teddy Tinling. 'The ultimate was that the Wimbledon committee handling the affair behaved so tactlessly on her arrival.'

Queen Mary and her entourage arrived exactly at 3pm. It was to have been a day of splendid tennis and the Queen was eagerly waiting to see her favourite play. The crowds were exhilarated as this was to be a game charged with personal emotions as well as expertise.

The Queen was seated in the royal box on the Centre Court. But where was Suzanne? She had not arrived at the courts the hour before a match as is usual. She was not in her hotel. She could not be found.

Half an hour later her taxi swept through the gates and there sat Suzanne, tense, pale, predatory. She was already in a high state of nerves for her match. The committee and staff were collected on the steps of the main entrance to meet her.

She was hustled into the committee room and severely reprimanded. As she was to complain later, she was not even asked to sit down. It is interesting to note that when Rosie Casals was chastised last year for flaunting a dress that distinctly reeked of advertising, she, too, was left standing. On such occasions the Wimbledon Committee Room becomes like a military courtroom.

On hearing the situation Suzanne Lenglen burst into floods of furious tears and rushed to her dressing-room locking the door behind her. The officials followed suit and listened petrified as they heard her wailing and beating her head in dull thuds against the wall. Would she knock herself senseless? Nothing like this had ever happened at Wimbledon before. Commander Hillyard and his successor, Major Larcombe, thought this must be stopped and sent messengers to try and find Borotra who was somewhere in the grounds. If anyone could reason with the demented Suzanne it was her countryman and devoted friend.

Borotra takes up the saga:

' "Jean, Jean, something terrible has happened. You must do something," Commander Hillyard said to me. "First of all Suzanne had kept her opponents waiting and secondly she is keeping Queen Mary. You must save the day. Even if she does play and she plays badly, she must put in an appearance on the court. *She must not disappoint the Queen.*"

'So you see what could I do. I went to the ladies' dressing-room and I put blinkers on my eyes. I do not remember if there was anyone else there. Probably not. But I, too, was nervous.

'I remained five minutes with her but it was useless. She was in a frenzy. She had the *crise de nerfs*. She said: "I can't. I can't. They should have advised me. I can't even stand on my feet. I am ill." '

Smiling sadly as it all came back, M Borotra shrugged his shoulders and said to me: 'When a woman says that, you can't force her. I came out and told them that she was physically and nervously unable to play. I did not even know the whole story until then. So the committee said:

' "There is only one thing you must do, Jean. You must go to Queen Mary. She will take it better from you than anyone else. You are Suzanne's friend and her partner in the mixed doubles. Go and explain and apologise."

'I can still see myself now going up the stairs to the royal box. Then the public seeing me appear there. Groundsmen to cover the delay had been pretending to prepare the courts by rolling them over and over but the public knew there was something wrong. Wimbledon crowds are very *sympathetique*. I did not kiss the Queen's hand. She had gloves on. But I told her the truth:

' "Your Majesty, I have just seen Suzanne Lenglen in her dressing-room and she has had a *crise de nerfs* and is absolutely unable to stand on her feet. She has it in her mind to apologise but at the moment she is unable to do so. She is very, very sorry."

'I could not tell her that it was not Suzanne's fault that she did not know of this early match.

'Queen Mary looked and was very sweet. She said: "I hope that she will be quite well very soon again. Give her my best wishes." '

By 5pm, the news agencies had the story on the wires all over the world . . . Suzanne had affronted the Queen. Every reporter fashioned the story according to his own whim. Suzanne was unobtainable to defend herself and there was no one there strong enough to advise her to meet the Press and clear herself as would happen today.

I can't for one moment see Billie Jean King believing that she was in the right, not standing up and defending herself in such a situation.

The only other player ever to be late on the Centre Court was the American Dinny Pails. In 1946 he was lost on the Underground and the Centre Court programme had to be switched. The bearded Dane Ullrich was also late for a match one year. He was found sitting on the floor in a public telephone box playing his guitar quietly to himself.

Suzanne's opponents all asked that her matches be postponed until the next day, and these were, in fact, played over the next few days. Suzanne's asthma had returned and she was playing badly. The public's mood was ugly. This was not how people behaved at Wimbledon. Their idol had fallen. Suzanne suffered it all. She was desolate, hurt and bewildered. Over the next few days she played in only half the matches scheduled, scratching when her nerve and health failed.

In her final doubles match against Elizabeth Ryan and Mary Browne, three times within a point of success, Suzanne was denied even this last victory. She and Didi Vlasto lost the match. When she left the court, the diamond pin fastening her bandeau, symbol of her new affluence, had come unfastened.

Even then there was more humiliation to come. The geography of the royal box is such that as the players come out of their dressing-room, they enter a foyer which has steps leading up to the Centre Court and eventually the royal box. It was, therefore, quite possible that as one of the royal family went past someone would have been coming in or out of the dressing-room.

It was at just such a place in the next few days that Queen Mary passed Suzanne. Suzanne dropped her curtsy but Queen Mary seemed to ignore it.

It had been planned that in this brilliant social year Suzanne was to be presented at court. Patou had made the dress. All France was aglow with pride, but after the royal affront, conferences were called at the French Embassy and in due course a story appeared in the Press that Mlle Lenglen had been advised by Mme de Fleurian, wife of the Ambassador, to withdraw her application to be presented.

Suzanne left London never again to play at Wimbledon. Several years later she arrived as an onlooker and when the crowds in the Centre Court heard that she was outside they left their seats and surged to have a look at Suzanne. For an hour she was bathed in her former glory.

So this is the story that has come down over the years about Suzanne. A piquant epilogue is that when Norah Gordon Cleather wrote her book *Wimbledon Story* twenty-one years later, she sent a copy to Queen Mary. She received a letter back from an equerry to say that she was utterly delighted to receive the book but only one thing she regretted was to find in it an account of an incident that was not true. She certainly would never deliberately shun Miss Suzanne Lenglen and if such a thing had happened, it could only be that she had passed her unnoticed. Was the royal memory reconciled or had it all been a mischievous mistake?

By then Suzanne Lenglen, the greatest woman player of all time, was dead. She had died of pernicious anaemia in Paris, aged thirty-nine, during Wimbledon Fortnight in 1938 after a long and painful illness.

Of all the people who spoke to me about Suzanne Lenglen, Teddy Tinling was the most revealing. He had known her from his early days in the South of France where he became her favourite umpire. He not only understood her as a woman but admired the Lenglen's pioneer attitude to professionalism.

'Suzanne's father had instilled in his daughter a philosophy that was already very much criticised in England at the time: "There is no point in playing if you can't win."

'It was his own personal philosophy that he had worked out when he was sweating it out in his five-day cycling races. If he saw clearly on the third day that he wasn't going to win he didn't see any point in continuing round the arena for the next two days to end up number nineteen. Though this is a philosophy that is accepted in the seventies, in the era that she projected it, it was considered very advanced thinking. It was regarded as a great defect in her character. Above all it was un-English.

'Her concept of sporting obligation was to give her spectators a complete exchange for what they were giving her. Her concept was more highly professional than most. In this she was comparable to Marlene Dietrich in her approach to her art.

'To me, her pattern of behaviour was more professional than if she had said: "I don't care if I lose." All her so-called tantrums, artistic temperament and so on were valid in their own way but to me they stemmed from her intense professionalism.

'In essence she was the first person in the world to appreciate that tennis at her level was part of show business. She envisaged this at a time when it was a sport and nothing but a sport. It was then merely the prerogative of the leisured classes.

'She foresaw patterns of tennis that will endure to the year 2000. There is hardly a thing that happens in tennis today, be it in professionalism or in the spectators' rights, that she did not anticipate and put into practice for herself. To me, she rates as a dazzling performer fifty years before her time.'

CHAPTER 7

The Greatest Doubles Player in the World

She strides through the Members' Enclosure with her halo of clotted cream hair, authoritative clear eyes roaming to catch the sight of friends, cotton dust coat floating behind. Heads turn.

This then is Elizabeth Ryan today, holder of more championships than anyone else at Wimbledon. A tennis giant if ever there was one and the finest women's doubles player the world has seen.

Of the nineteen titles she won at Wimbledon seven were in the mixed doubles and twelve in the ladies' doubles and although she won the national singles championship in nine countries the Wimbledon title always eluded her. She was dogged by incredible bad luck.

Elizabeth ('Bunny') Ryan's Wimbledon career stretches back over half a century. She has partnered most of the legendary names to success—Suzanne Lenglen, Helen Wills Moody, Mme Mathieu, Jack Crawford. She won her first Wimbledon championship in 1914 and her last in 1934, spanning twenty years.

Her statistics in the Guinness book of records are formidable. She won the national doubles championship in twenty-two countries and the national singles in nine countries including Russia where she caught one of the last trains out in 1914.

Oddly enough, 'Bunny' Ryan never intended to be a tennis

player, for she meant to train as a concert pianist and study in Germany. The two Ryan sisters, Alice and Elizabeth, of California, arrived in Britain as schoolgirls to stay with friends in Devon. They had both played a little tennis in America but it was not until their mother decided that the vast quantities of Devonshire cream they consumed were bad for puppy-fat that she sent them to have regular daily exercise. 'Bunny' was a natural. She had the power and concentration that championship tennis required. While her sister took up golf 'Bunny' made her way to Wimbledon.

'I attribute becoming first class in tennis to taking off my girdle,' she says today. Tennis experts class her mighty 'chop' as one of the greatest displays of individual style that Wimbledon has ever seen.

Together with Suzanne Lenglen they achieved wonders. Suzanne, the delicate ballerina with her graceful fluid movements, backed up by 'Bunny' Ryan's brilliant solidarity and crashing strength. An incongruous pair, the likes of which Wimbledon has never seen since. 'Bunny' used to raise her arms to heaven before serving which became known as her 'Invocation to the Gods'.

Of Suzanne 'Bunny' Ryan says today:

'She was a genius. With that great long stride of hers. She took the ball early and her arms seemed to be frightfully long coming into my side of the court all the time. We knew exactly what each other was doing. We had no need to talk. The fact that we spoke very little to each other on court did not matter. We only had to step on the court and we were instinctive partners.'

In her early days at Wimbledon 'Bunny' Ryan was invariably drawn against the invincible Suzanne Lenglen in her early rounds. Like everyone else she hadn't a chance. In 1924 Suzanne withdrew from Wimbledon, but not before she had put Elizabeth Ryan out and thus deprived her of an almost certain chance to win the title. The next chance was in the early thirties.

'Along came the next giant, Helen Wills Moody. During my time she won five times. The only time she wasn't there I hurt my

D

Achilles tendon in Paris and couldn't play for three months. It took me a long time to be reconciled that I wasn't going to win Wimbledon and I can tell you it really hurt.'

Miss Ryan retired from Wimbledon on winning the ladies' doubles with Mme Mathieu in 1934 and turned professional.

'I went to the greatest teacher in the world Mrs Dudley Larcombe and asked her to teach me everything she knew.

'I spent about £150 with her two hours a day learning how to teach. I told her I was going to California to teach hence she said she would help me.'

From then on Elizabeth Ryan spent many happy years teaching at the Royal Hawaiian Hotel in Honolulu, the Carib Hilton in Puerto Rico, the Del Monte Hotel at Pebble Beach near San Francisco, and the Huntington Hotel in Pasadena, as well as many private schools and colleges. From schoolchildren to movie stars—they have all been her pupils. People waited a year to get on her teaching list.

Her teaching axiom was like herself—straightforward and to the point.

'As a sunflower blossoms with the sun your pupils must bloom with encouragement.'

Last year on 26 August, Elizabeth Ryan, who now lives in England with her sister, rounded off her splendid career. After a celebration luncheon party at the home of the American tennis enthusiast J. van Alen at Newport, flanked by the one-time blustery, raw-speaking Gardnar Mulloy and 'Bitsy' Grant, who had also played at Wimbledon, she was presented with the golden medal of the National Lawn Tennis Hall of Fame.

'To honour Elizabeth Ryan, enshrined 26 August 1972' were the simple words on the back.

The full circle of America honouring its greatest Wimbledon champion had been completed.

CHAPTER 8

The Two Helens

T he competitors' lounge at the All England Club is the meat market of world tennis. It is next to the referees' office on the first floor and overlooks court number 3. It is a bustling mixture of players' workroom, club, restaurant and gossip shop. From 1pm onwards until after 8pm it is a meeting place where the tennis world meets to 'chew the fat'. On fine evenings the players overspill on to the roof garden where you can sit with the All England Club spread beneath you like a giant jigsaw puzzle. The colours are paint-box bright—green, red, blue, yellow—constantly changing patterns like a kaleidoscope.

If there are tensions or jealousies they are well concealed. The Americans especially have a standard temperament grafted on to them by their astute professional coaches. They sit in huddles discussing prize money, the best buys at Marks and Spencer, the best pills to take for air sickness, each other's form and 'the circuit' because they are all on a circuit of some sort.

Goolagong has lost her world championship and sits sipping orange with Jennifer Edwards, daughter of her legal guardian and coach Vic Edwards. She is relaxed, laughing. Only the dark shadows under her eyes show the strain and pressure she has been under the last fortnight.

Billie Jean King enters, gesticulating, teasing, noisy, happy and immensely confident. She has just achieved what she set out to do —the Wimbledon hat-trick. On court she has a dour unswerving determination to eliminate everything and everyone around her. To win. Off court, in sleek fitting orange jeans and brilliant shirt she looks smaller, more feminine and vulnerable. She melts into the jostling, babbling room of people. Evert passes, a neat little seventeen-year-old, honey gold hair and skin. Only her eyes are cool. Close-set, steel-cold eyes that mark her a dedicated champion.

It is all so different from those pre-war days of the two Helens —Wills Moody and Jacobs. That clash of temperament that kept Wimbledon crowds on their toes. There are no scenes today. The most a loser does is have a cry in her bath with a cup of tea.

'They haven't got the personality like the old ones,' someone remarked to me. 'Remember those two Helens and the fun we all had watching their vendetta. Along with their strokes it seems that even their emotions have been processed.'

Like Chris Evert, Helen Wills was still a schoolgirl when she first came to Wimbledon from America in 1924. At seventeen in 1923 she had beaten Kathleen ('Kitty') McKane, Britain's great hope, at the new Forest Hills tournament, and the next year the American champion Mrs Mallory. Wimbledon awaited her with that extraordinary mixture that it still has today of reserve, admiration, expectation and condemnation.

For her first appearance at Wimbledon Helen Wills arrived in her school uniform—a stiff white skirt and middy blouse—and accompanied by her mother. She was *gauche* with remnants of schoolgirl puppy-fat. Only the eyeshade and aloof, ice-cool manner, which were to become her signature, were in evidence. To Wimbledon fans the eyeshade was as much a bombshell as 'Gussy' Moran's lace panties, but to practical Helen it was merely her defence against the harsh light of the Californian tennis courts where she did her practice. But such was its impact that for years to come schoolgirls round the world adopted the 'Helen Wills' eyeshade' just as the Lenglen bandeaux had caught on several years before.

In the twenties Helen Wills was called 'Little Poker Face', much as Chris Evert, who is a natural comparison, was dubbed 'Little Miss Icicle' last year at Wimbledon.

Norah Gordon Cleather, personal assistant to the secretary of the All England Club, who was to get to know Helen well, described her:

'In her early tournaments as a schoolgirl, Helen Wills had been afraid of becoming "too tired" to carry out the vigorous baseline tactics on which her game was based, and we learned that even as a junior she had carried her economy of effort policy to an extreme.

'Sure enough, not only did this solemn girl consider it a waste of strength to make an ejaculation or show any expression of feeling when she played, but sometimes she decided that the energy she would sacrifice in running for a shot would be altogether too extravagant and she would stand quite still and refuse to run at all.

'It was this very "immobility" that in another way earned her the description "Little Poker Face", and the nickname was most apt as it was impossible to tell from her expression whether she was nervous, pleased, or just plain bored when she was playing.'

In her first Wimbledon final Helen Wills found herself up against the steadiness of top ranking English girl Kitty McKane, who played under the name of Biddy Godfree after her marriage. Years later Helen Wills is reported to have said that this was the most gruelling match she ever had; it was the only occasion during her many years of playing at Wimbledon that the mask came off, and after the match she sobbed in the dressing-room.

Today, forty-eight years later, sun-tanned, grey-haired, athletic and vital, Biddy Godfree still plays tennis at Wimbledon during the summer months. We talked of that now famous match:

'I always played better when I was behind in my matches. I don't know why but something seemed to happen when I was losing and in both the finals—1924 with Helen Wills and 1926 against the Spanish star Senorita de Alvarez—I was a set down and 4-1 down in the second set and then I can remember saying to myself, "Well, what you are doing is obviously no good, you're playing a losing game, you've got to change all this before it's too late. Go for things, go for lines, for shots and so on."

'Luckily it paid off. It is a very nerve-racking feeling for an opponent to be well ahead and then suddenly the opponent you think is almost beaten to turn round and come surging forward.

'Helen Wills was a very deep concentrator. It was her great strength. At the end of the match with me, she said, "Thank you very much," and then looking up at the umpire thanked him very much and said:

' "What was the scoring in that set?"

'I think it was very extraordinary not to know what the score was because you play to the score anyhow. I think the applause was very much for the English person that time and there is no doubt about it that everybody all round obviously wanting you to win is a terrific boost to your morale.'

And of her match in 1926:

'Lili de Alvarez was elegant and beautiful and a wonderful half volleyer from the baseline but on this occasion it is only fair to say I think that she ran out of steam towards the end of the third set. She got tired—that was her weakness and she was a light-hearted player. On court in her very pretty dresses she was one of the most fascinating of players of all time to watch. I am sure Suzanne Lenglen was the greatest of them all but I am not sure about Alice Marble. She won the triple crown at Wimbledon in 1939 and if it had not been for the war years she may have gone on winning for a very long time.'

When Mrs Godfree and the Comtesse de la Valdene, as Lili had become, met at Wimbledon three years ago, they talked over that final in 1926. As the Englishwoman remembers:

'She told me that the very morning of the match she had just heard from the man she had expected to marry that it was, in fact, off. Who could play tennis after that sort of news?'

Helen Wills returned to Wimbledon the following year to win the first of her eight Wimbledon titles, making her the record title-holder for the women's singles. Once again, it was the fiery Spaniard on the Centre Court but this time the American out-stripped her.

Dan Maskell remembers the arrival of Helen Wills Moody with the clarity of a professional.

'My first appearance on the courts as a coach at the All England Club was when I was twenty years of age. Three months before I had put my foot through a washbasin at Queen's and practically cut my big toe off. Knowing that I was going to Wimbledon and in order to keep in form I used to stand with my foot in plaster up against a wall knocking up to keep my eye in.

'I was in this condition still bandaged up and Helen Wills Moody had just arrived from Australia and was anxious to get some practice after the five weeks on the boat. The photographers were all there as her arrival was part of the mystique of Wimbledon. This beautiful woman did not reveal any feelings on the cout- but with people she liked she was a very warm person. In her bre guiling Californian drawl, she congratulated me on getting the job and then we got down to business.

'One of the interesting things about Helen Wills Moody is that she used to have a set practice piece. She would practise for fifteen minutes or so to get warmed up and get her eye in and then she would say: "Dan, we will now play our usual two sets."

'These two usual sets meant that I would play like a very good woman player. I was not allowed to run in on my serve because very few women did then and it was a baseline game and I wasn't allowed to drop shot unless it was an absolute obvious one. I played from about 5ft or more outside the baselines and I used to win something like 6–4, 7–5. I never dropped a set and she was fully extended. Then we used to stop for a breather and she would say:

' "Shall we finish off and you have some fun."

'This meant that I could play one set exactly as I liked. I could come in behind my serve, drop shots, slice, chop, in fact play like a man against her. This had some sense apart from being nice to me, as she enjoyed being harassed out of her normal tempo by a man's game. She had developed the rhythm and control at a pace to which she was accustomed and now suddenly she had to adapt, compensate and use all her game and ball sense to play against something far faster than she would get. I used to enjoy these games with her as much as I used to enjoy playing against

Borotra. She was so appreciative of everything that I did for her.'

Off court this great beauty with her porcelain skin, near perfect features and pale luminous eyes, lived like the great star she was. Her clothes came from Paris, she always travelled with a dressing-case fitted with crystal bottles with gold stoppers, and steadfastly refused to share the car and chauffeur allotted her to Wimbledon with any other player. In the dressing-room she was aloof, scarcely ever spoke to the other players and was arrogant with the staff.

It is doubtful whether her behaviour would have been tolerated at Wimbledon today. Perhaps even more than Suzanne Lenglen, she knew her own value and prized it. Helen Wills not only won the Wimbledon title eight times but captured the American four and French twice.

Helen Jacobs was quite a different type of woman. Quiet with a classical Greek head that was the delight of the photographers, she lacked the panache of 'Big Helen' but among Wimbledon fans had her own fanatic following. When she finally won the championship in 1936, she was one of the most popular champions ever.

It seems odd that Wimbledon should have been the place where these two dissimilar girls from neighbouring streets in the same suburb of Berkeley, California chose to enact their own private and public vendettas. Though they rarely spoke on or off the court, they were to meet in four finals at Wimbledon, and Helen Wills to win them all.

Their final meeting remains one of the most poignant pre-war memories. Impeccable in white, Helen Wills Moody took to the court confidently, her face frozen into a sphinx-like calm under the eye shadow. Helen Jacobs wore her usual boyish shorts.

'Big Helen' applied her usual impassive concentration as 'Little Helen' began playing with her ankle bandaged against a sprain she had got in practising. Helen Jacobs began playing at the peak of her form until suddenly she gave a cry of pain as she leapt for an overhead shot. The crowd, so desperately wishing her to win, began to murmur nervously as she doubled up in agony. Helen

Wills Moody took out her handkerchief and quietly blew her nose.

The game continued as Helen Wills Moody hammered home her shots. There was no pity, no consideration as she sent her shots scorching the sidelines from left to right. The crowd watched in stunned and horrified silence as the score reached 4–4 in the first set.

At the end of the next game, Helen Jacobs was clearly distressed as her leg had begun to swell and the bandage was pinching her. She asked Helen Wills during a change over of ends if she would mind if she stopped. Knowing Helen Wills' concentration, it is highly unlikely that she even heard, but the fact that she did not even bother to stop infuriated the crowd.

Later, at Mrs Wightman's insistence, the umpire stopped the game while Helen Jacobs removed the bandage. The leg was worse. Mrs Wightman begged Helen Jacobs to scratch, but she refused. She limped through the remainder of the match without collecting another game.

With the fascination of a spider watching a fly in her web, Helen Wills Moody finished off her victim. Wimbledon was shocked.

In his autobiography *My Story* published in 1948, Tilden revealed with shattering frankness the rivalry of these two great players:

'Helen Jacobs summed everything up for me the following day when she said: "You know, Bill, I don't mind her being a so-and-so, but I object to her being a stupid so-and-so. If she had only smiled when she shook hands at the end and said, 'I'm glad you broke your damn leg'—or something like that, then no one would have known how she really felt." '

CHAPTER 9

Power Game from
America

It was the Americans who brought to Wimbledon the power
game as we know it today—the devastating serving volleyer,
the ball that feels like a ton weight when it shudders on to the
racket and the receiver has to grip his racket tighter to resist its
ferocity.

It was an entirely new conception of tennis after the sophisticated, witty techniques of the French era and was to change the
pace of tennis in the future. The style that Stan Smith, Ken Rosewall and John Newcombe have today is a heritage from this
brilliant period in lawn tennis.

For the first time in the history of the All England Club, 1930
brought an all-American victory except for the mixed doubles
which Jack Crawford of Australia won with Elizabeth Ryan.
W. H. ('Big Bill') Tilden using the power game he had developed
after nine long years broke the period of French supremacy in his
spectacular semi-final with Borotra.

The overnight queues for this great match looked different from
today's untidy scene. The women were chic in pleated skirts and
Clara Bow cloches, and the men in sombre suits and felt hats.
But there the formality stopped. They were there to enjoy themselves and the mood was infinitely gayer. They fox-trotted to
portable gramophones, sang, set up tables and chairs and played

bridge, or did crossword puzzles. And when the gates opened, they rushed to the dressing-room entrance of the All England Club to see their gods arrive. Hunch-shouldered with all his star quality, Tilden, immaculate in a snow-white suit with navy spotted cravat and buckskin shoes. Borotra, the tennis pierrot, his beret saucily tilted at a rakish angle.

Play began and Tilden was soon in his stride mixing his cannon-ball service with a moderated 'kicking' one. Borotra pounced like a panther on anything short over his head. He always played a gay game and that day his exuberance was electrifying.

At one point Tilden had appealed to the umpire that Borotra was taking too long to change ends, thus sneaking a short rest. The umpire had chastised Borotra who from then on barged from one end of the court to the other like a naughty child, changing berets *en route*, flinging his towel at a bewildered ball boy, chuckling quietly to himself. The clowning was highly effective but it did not help him to win the match. Tilden had shown a new kind of power game, and Wimbledon players and followers realised that they were witnessing the birth of a new era in tennis.

Bill Tilden has always been regarded as the all-time great.

'When my wife saw him for the first time, she said, "Now I have seen a real champion," ' remembers 'Bunny' Austin. 'When I first played against him—it was in a double—and he certainly gave me the impression I didn't exist, or at best was merely a small fly which could be easily swatted by his cannon-ball service.

'He had a tremendous serve—the first hit flat and with cannon-ball speed. At one time at a crucial moment in a Davis Cup double he took four balls in his hand and served four aces, totally unnerving the opposition. His second serve was a spin. He had powerful flat drives on either wing and the complete control of cutting and slice. But he was not a great volleyer and though he could move with speed across the court he was slower in moving forwards and backwards, and it was this weakness the French exploited when they took the Davis Cup from America in 1927, after the Americans had won it for eight years.'

The fact that Tilden had had a finger amputated from his

racket hand, due to blood poisoning, in no way detracted from his mighty game. He merely revised his grip and certain shots in his repertoire to overcome the weakness.

Everything about Tilden from his bitchy unsporting remarks which he occasionally made to his advice to young players was larger than life. Always eat your lunch two hours before a match, he wrote in his book, yet 'Bunny' Austin distinctly remembers him eating veal and a good helping of spaghetti followed by apple pie before picking up his racket and saying: 'Well, I guess I gotta play my match.' He was quite a heavy smoker, too, in contrast to people like Borotra who didn't drink or smoke.

After his win over Borotra, Tilden had a relatively easy one over his fellow-countryman, Wilmer Allison. It was an astonishing performance for a thirty-eight-year-old.

Two years previously he had left the court after his great fight with Cochet who beat him and turned as if to say good-bye to that cherished piece of turf. His comment to the Press when asked about next year was:

'Ah, but I am thirty-six. Still Wimbledon is Wimbledon.'

And here he was back at thirty-eight, playing like a genius.

Ellsworth Vines, twenty-one-year-old Californian, smashed and crashed his way to the top at his first Wimbledon. His match with W. H. 'Bunny' Austin remains one of the most devastatingly brutal defeats in Wimbledon history. If anyone could explain the phenomenon of the American power game it was Austin. We talked about it in the sitting-room of his charming house in Victoria Square in London. At that time Austin had ranked as Number 2 player in the world, just behind Tilden, and was the first Englishman to have reached the final at Wimbledon for many years.

'Vines was a better player than I, so let's get that straight. I knew this, but I was in good condition and my mother who dabbled in astrology had cast my horoscope that morning and said I was bound to win!

'When we started, however, I knew that something had gone wrong in the stars. We both began badly and the score mounted slowly. In the first set I lost my service and finally the set 6–4. In the second set Vines played much better and began to get his cannon-ball service working and again I lost the set 6–2. At that time I still had faith in the stars. As the third set started it was like encountering a 150 mile an hour hurricane. I was being totally flattened. I simply could not see Vines' services nor could I see his returns to my services. The score mounted rapidly against me, 1–0, 2–0, 3–0, 4–0 and 5–0, and on his own service he reached match point 40–15.

'I stood there waiting for Vines to serve watching for his smooth, rhythmic, powerful swing. I waited. I did not move. I saw nothing, only a puff of dust on my service court and then the sound of a ball hitting the stop-netting behind me. Vines had won. I have never believed in astrology since that day.'

It was the most consistent display of power, plus accuracy that the Wimbledon fans had seen to date. Vines constantly hit the lines with those unreturnable serves and drives. He had packed away thirty aces in his twelve service games, winning the match with that final blinding ball.

There was deafening applause as this lanky 6ft 4in hero with the quiet demeanour of Stan Smith left the court. He played like a champion. He behaved like a champion. The Centre Court connoisseurs were well-satisfied. Here was a new era of speed and excitement.

It is interesting in relating to the power game the subterfuges that these American players resorted to in order to gain sufficient strength to continue their exhausting method of playing. For instance, Vines and Co could ruthlessly rush about the court hammering home their devastating shots but having won the point return to their position like astronauts on a lunar walk. They intrigued the crowds and infuriated their opponents who were kept waiting between services.

This necessity for taking frequent 'breathers' is accepted as part and parcel of Wimbledon tennis today. As I watched Stan Smith in last year's finals with Nastase, he employed his own version of resting—taking a long time to towel-up. The intimacy of television brings this immensely human aspect of tennis candidly into focus.

The year Vines lost to Australia's Jack Crawford, Crawford went to Dan Maskell the night before at 7pm for some practice.

'Dan, I am playing someone tomorrow who will slice heavily. Will you give me an idea of it?' Crawford asked. 'I want you to come out and really bang your forehand and it doesn't matter whether it goes in or out but knock it as hard as you like. I have to stand up against Ellsworth's forehand tomorrow. Just give me a bashing.'

Maskell remembers: 'I was hitting this ball like mad, like Vines throwing his weight forward. Jack fenced them with his glorious sliced backhand. I made mistakes because it wasn't my method of play or my stroke. But I thought: "This man is playing damn well, damn well. He is quiet in his mind. He is confident. He is not really embarrassed by anything. He can cope with it all. My God, I think this man could win it." '

Quarter of an hour later just as Maskell was changing his shirt, Vines went into the dressing-room. Could he spare a little time?

'I told him I'd love to. I was a bit tired but no matter. Ellsworth said to me: "I saw you having a knock with Jack. Wonder if you would come and hit some backhand slices at me."

'We went out and I thought: "My God, this man is having difficulty with his forehand," and I was beginning to see the vulnerability of this really flat forehand. In the end, without saying anything, Vines stopped crashing this forehand and started to lift it into my backhand corner and come in and finish it on the volley. I thought, "This is obviously going to be his tactics. He will start trying to knock Jack off the court with sheer power. If he has difficulty with the low ball I can see what he will do. He will go into the backhand and try and win his points on the volley." Up to a point this is what happened.

'The interesting thing about this is that as I came off the court with Ellsworth a man came up to me who I had not seen in years, S. Wallace Merehew, a great old man who used to run a monthly magazine *American Tennis*.

'He said: "Dan, I have just been watching this performance with Ellsworth and Jack. Who is going to win?"

'I said that if I had a bet I think I would make it on Jack.

'He said: "Why?"

'I said: "Jack seems to be happier in mind. He is not worried about any of his shots. He will go into the match on the instinct level. Ellsworth will go in on the conscious level. He is a bit concerned about the low ball and he knows that he is going to have a lot off Jack." '

Jack Crawford did win after an epic match even though Ellsworth Vines was at that time the great exponent of the power game. His strategy was more cunning.

Among the other American power exponents was Donald Budge. There are some people at Wimbledon today who say that he was the greatest player that lived. He had everything. This gangling, jolly, freckle-faced Huckleberry Finn with his marmalade hair and boyish charm had been a baseball player in California before turning to tennis. The only vulnerability that Budge had was if he could be caught in his deep forehand corner. If a player managed to do this then his forehand was in danger.

Among the most stylish of the American power game exponents was Sidney Wood, who arrived at Wimbledon in 1927, aged fifteen and straight from school. He broke current traditions by insisting that he play in white knickerbockers and golf stockings.

Frank Shields, the most handsome man ever to play at Wimbledon, was another human power-house. Looking down from his 6ft 3in height, this Californian Adonis had up till then perhaps the greatest slice service that the world had seen. A hard cannonball service but a slice service, that swung in the air and broke right away. His opponents had to almost stand outside the court to take it. When he swung into the right court from underneath the royal box on the Centre Court, he could swing his serve to hit the sideline and his opponent was way out between the doubles line and the crowd. Shields was not a great stylist but a tremendously effective player. He was typical of the American power game

players who were not all great tennis players but had two important shots perfected—the big volley and big serve.

Wilmer L. Allison was another of the American power-playing
crowd. With his very powerful service he followed in each time.
He was one of the greatest doubles players of all time and won
the championship three times.

All these players laid a foundation for the modern game we see
today, whether it is played in the huge tennis arenas of Texas or
on the gentle lawns of Wimbledon.

Page 65
(*right*) Jean Borotra
(France), the 'Bounding
Basque' and the greatest
showman of Wimbledon;
(*below*) Stan Smith (USA),
winner of the 1972 men's
singles. He 'asked God for
help'

Page 66
(*above*) Suzanne Lenglen
(France) and Queen Mary.
They both loved Wimble-
don and gave much to the
game; (*left*) Maria Bueno
(Brazil), the most graceful
champion since Lenglen.
She won the title three
times

CHAPTER 10

Homespun Champions

F red Perry and Dorothy Round were the toasts of Wimbledon in 1934—the year they brought the championship
back to Britain. They were the kind of homespun stars
that the Wimbledon crowd appreciate.

She was the Sunday-school teacher from Dudley in the Midlands
and he was the self-taught rough shot from Eastbourne. And both
had come up the hard way.

For Dorothy it had meant the kind of superhuman effort that
Wimbledon inspires in her third set against Helen Jacobs of
America and for Fred, a performance of sheer dynamism in his
game against Australia's 'Gentleman' Jack Crawford.

'I guess I was the first Englishman to bring the American attitude to the game of lawn tennis,' Perry explained to me.

'I learnt that way back in 1930 when I went to America for the
first time. The captain of the Davis Cup, L. A. Godfree, called
me into his cabin and said:

' "Now look here. We're going to be in America six weeks.
We are going to play six or seven tournaments. We don't expect
you to be in the tournament after the first day, but don't worry
about it. But if I look out on the tennis courts any day during
any of the following weeks and I don't see you either watching or
practising, you go back to England on the first boat."

'In America the big thing is that you want to go hit something.
So I used to walk around in my tennis clothes with a racket all

the time and ask everyone, "Do you want a hit?" I'd just hit balls until they came out of my ears and in that two months in America I changed my game completely. I got the American attitude of never wanting to be second. When I played I went out there to come in first and I think a lot of English people didn't understand or realise that in those days.'

In the thirties Perry, a former world champion table tennis player, was inclined to be irrational, fractious, highly strung, temperamental, volatile. He was not the easiest player to handle and had a packet of mannerisms that were decidedly unnerving to his umpires. But he worked hard and had the will power to turn himself into a champion.

'I think it all goes back to probably round about 1925 or so when I first saw the game played in Eastbourne. I saw all these cars in Devonshire Park and went back to my father and he said:

' "Where have you been?"

'And I said, "I've been watching people play tennis. What are all those cars around there?"

' "People who play tennis," he said.

' "Well, if they can have cars like that, that's for me."

'I think I first came to Wimbledon to watch in 1928 in the standing room. I couldn't afford anything else but I enjoyed it. The following year I qualified at Roehampton and got through two rounds. But 1930 was my lucky year because in the third round on the Wednesday I had to play the number four seed, an Italian, in the singles on court number 3. In the members' room above, overlooking that court, they had a selection committee meeting for a team of four men to go to America in August and a team of three men and two women to go to South America in the autumn. They had all the teams selected except one and they had adjourned the meeting to watch our game. After I won three sets to one they decided that the name of Perry should be included in that team.

'That was the start. You have to have the breaks when you need them and that was my day. I retained the title for three successive summers when I quit and went to America as a professional.

I came back to England in about '48 or '49 and I've come here every year since.'

At the finish of the Davis Cup Challenge Round in 1936, Perry waited behind when all the crowds had gone home. He and Norah Gordon Cleather walked out on to the Centre Court.

'Let me stay here a moment by myself,' he asked. He knew then that he would never again play at Wimbledon.

I asked Perry about Centre Court nerves and whether, even with his self-confidence, he had ever suffered from them.

'I'll never forget that first time I went out on to the Centre Court. It is an ordeal for anybody because you come out from behind a barrier. When I played for the first time on the Centre Court it was with Dr Gregory, the old English Davis Cup player. I got through somehow to the last sixteen and the referee, Mr F. R. Burrow said:

' "I'd like you to come down early because I want to take you on the Centre Court personally."

'So I came down about twelve o'clock, there was nobody around and he walked me out on to the Centre Court. We quietly stood in the middle and he said:

' "I want you to stay here four or five minutes and get the feel of the place."

'It is different because it has the largest area of grass in the world which is completely surrounded by a covered stand. That's the one problem here. They can't build it any higher otherwise the grass would die. They can't even get the roller out now as it was there before the stands were built.

'There are so many things like that around here. I like it. It's Wimbledon. But I remember I stood out there on that Centre Court for about ten to fifteen minutes getting the feel of it and going from one end to the other to get an idea because with the long background of the darkened stands you haven't got the sun on bright shirts, or bright dresses and white things like that. It's dark so you see the ball quicker and for a longer period of time until you're used to it. It's quite different. You see the ball longer but it flies at you all of a sudden.

'When King George V and Queen Mary walked in on that final's day we had to stop and let them sit down, and bow. I had never seen them before and bowing to royalty was then some new experience for the son of a Labour MP. I lost that set and then, I think, they went out for tea and I began to get better and they came back again and that was the end of the match as far as I was concerned. But it was a great experience.

'I think the fact that Mr Burrow took me out there just to get used to it is something I was forever grateful for, because the next time I went out there was no problem at all.'

Captain Mike Gibson, the present referee, does in fact arrange for all probable champions to have at least one game on the Centre Court before the finals, and Princess Marina instituted the practice to be detained on the staircase until a game was over so that she did not interrupt play.

When Fred Perry won the championship in 1934 he was the first Englishman to have won it since 1909 when A. W. Gore was the title-holder. The men's singles had been played on the Friday as they were then. The Friday evening paper posters carried only one word 'Fred'. To this day he has kept one as a souvenir.

'I don't know how the champions celebrate now but I had a real night out with some friends. We lived in Ealing in those days. I can't remember the details at all, but we had dinner and did a theatre and everywhere we went everything was on the house. I don't know how I got there but I ended up at the Grand Hotel at Eastbourne next morning in white tie and tails.

'I was still wearing them when the secretary of the All England came on the 'phone—God knows how he found us—and said, "The King and Queen want to meet you. You've GOT to be at Wimbledon this afternoon." We were driven back and I know I wasn't looking too good. My father brought a suit down for me and I think they shaved me in the locker room. Dorothy and I had to go up there to the royal box and be presented and everyone had to stand up. King George V took one look at me and said:

' "You know as long as I'm standing up, Mr Perry, all the people have to stand up. Don't you think we should sit down."

'Which was a very good thing for me. He then said that he owed me an apology.

' "You see it is the first time since I have been king and on the throne that an Englishman has won Wimbledon and I was not here to see it, but I hope that you will appreciate that I have other things to do."

'Which I thought was quite something.'

As Dorothy Round and Fred Perry stood in the royal box 17,000 spectators applauded and great sound waves of clapping ricocheted round the wooden structure.

Even in Fred Perry's day psychology played an important part in championship tennis.

'I was never interested in what a tennis player could do on court,' says Perry today.

'I was interested in his mannerisms, his idiosyncrasies, his nervous motions. Jack Crawford had one trick I used to watch for. He used to wipe his hands like every other player does down the side of his pants, but when he got a bit nervous he'd wipe his hand across his chest and wiping a wet hand on a wet shirt doesn't do much good. I knew then that I had got him, that he was a bit nervous, and I'd get right after him.

'I mean if a man was nervous you'd just rush the heck out of him. That was all there was to it. Never gave him a chance to think. I really believe that I was the first Englishman to bring that home to England. If you get a man down, don't help him up, just stamp on his face. I think that is probably one of the main points that I had.'

Dorothy Round is now a comfortable no-nonsense, jolly housewife and every year she comes back to Wimbledon. Living in the Midlands she has only played once since the war at the All England Club but she continued her tennis up till 1970. Like so many other tennis players golf became her second sport which she still plays.

Did she also suffer from Centre Court nerves?

'Yes, not particularly Centre Court. Just nerves. Period. All I remember winning the championship is really the heat, the boiling heat. The umpire thought I had gone mad because I said to him when I crossed over once: "Oh, I do feel cold." He thought the sun had affected me.

'I think the most nervous match I ever had was playing Kay Stammers which was the first time she had played here. The first person I saw when I got on the court was my old headmistress who frightened me to death at school and frightened me even more sitting on the sideline.

'It seems to me on looking back that "match point" meant much more in those days than it does now. I mean people get match points now and lose them and then the match. In my day if we lost a match when we had match point it was an absolute tragedy, an absolute disaster. But how much of that is due to the fact that they make screaming winners now whereas we used to play possibly a little more painstakingly.'

In these pampered days of tennis training, Dorothy Round's early days are Spartan in comparison. She was totally dedicated from the time she was just a small girl.

'I resent the idea that we didn't train or take our tennis seriously,' she says today.

Her father and three brothers took care of her physical fitness. In dismantling a garage Dorothy Round's father, a building contractor, found two enormous doors and put them up at the bottom of the tennis court in the garden.

'I used to practise my volley against these because you can increase the speed of your reflexes against a wall very quickly. After that I used to run round the court twenty-five times for a mile.

'Actual practice meant a mile walk to the train from where we lived in Dudley, then the train and then the tram. And you still had to get back after playing. Most of my training was done against men in Birmingham during their lunch hours. One man in particular was most helpful as he played a bit like a woman. He played from the baseline and didn't rush up to the net.

'I love Patti Hogan's story of her idea of training was that she went to bed at 3.30am and not 5.30am. I didn't drink. I didn't smoke. I didn't do anything they do today. No, I was a very good girl. I don't know if I would be the same today and I don't know if I would have been such a good tennis player, but you never can tell, can you?'

Dorothy's tricolene tennis dresses were often home made and cost about 12s 6d. And when as a seventeen-year-old she began competing in tournaments, her mother went too.

'Looking back I think probably it was a bad thing. I ought to have been pushed out on my own. I was apt to think:

' "Oh, Mother's here. I must go home with Mother!"

'The first time I came up on my own to play at Wimbledon I stayed in a girls' club in Earl's Court and paid 32s 6d a week for bed and breakfast and dinner, and all meals at the weekend. Hot baths were 2d extra.'

For the champions like Dorothy Round the magic of Wimbledon is that it is made up of fragile, intimate memories. It is not only the glory of the Centre Court that matters.

'Originally there were two dressing-rooms and then there was the members'. The dressing-room downstairs where you started off was called, and still is, "the rabbit warren", and then you went upstairs when you graduated to being a better player.

'When I used to come here as an eighteen-year-old for three days' coaching with Dan Maskell of an hour a day, I used to use the upstairs room. There were little locker rooms with glass doors and on one of them was written "The Ladies' Champion". We all took it in turns, you see, to change in there just to say: "I'm the ladies' champion." I loved using it and used to think what a thrill if I ever got into it in my own right.

'By the time I was champion someone had obliterated it and by then, anyway, all the VIP players went up to the members' room. So I never did change in that little room as a champion.'

Comparisons were bound to come up. Did Dorothy Round think that the big money of today influences the spirit of the game?

'It meant just as much to us to win. I'm sure it did. I said to

Pip Jones (husband of Ann Jones who won for England in 1970) a little while ago:

' "Did winning £1,000 make any difference to Ann?"

'And he said, "It didn't make any difference at all."

'I don't think that I believe that. I got about £15 and a medal. I bought all the family silver table napkin rings which they still have today, and "Pop" Summers, who worked for Slazengers and looked after our rackets and things and took us to tournaments, a silver cigarette box.'

Dorothy Round was married in 1937 in London.

'Teddy Tinling offered to make my wedding dress before Wimbledon and I said that I didn't think I could afford it. But after I had won he got quite a bit of publicity so in the end I didn't have to pay for it anyway. Oyster brocade with silver threads in it. He made it beautifully and it had about a thousand teeny, weeny little buttons all with proper little buttonholes to put them in, all the way down the back.'

After she went to America during the war, she turned professional and was unable to play at Wimbledon again. But even professional players in the forties had more independence than they do today.

'I shouldn't like it if someone said to me, "You've got to go and play here."

'I should have said, "No, I'd rather play there." '

A practising Christian, Dorothy Round still does not approve of tennis on Sunday. In 1933 when she was playing at Forest Hills in America, the finals were played on Sundays. No one had told Dorothy this and after much excitement, the American officials agreed not to ask her to break her principles. Torrential rain averted the crisis and Dorothy played on the Monday.

'And I would still stick to my religious principles again today.

'In 1963 I was over in the USA coaching at an American summer camp. While flying from Boston to Cleveland to watch the Wightman Cup, the stewardess said to me:

' "Oh, you're English, aren't you? I've just been over in England watching the tennis at Wimbledon."

' "Isn't that a funny thing because so have I. I just left yester-day."

'Being conceited I had to tell her who I was, and a gentleman sitting behind said:

' "I must introduce myself. I'm Virginia Wade's father." '

CHAPTER 11

The Champion Who Never Was

One face that is absent during 'The Fortnight' is that of W. H. ('Bunny') Austin. He was called 'the Nijinsky of the courts', because of his astonishing gracefulness, and was one of the greatest lawn tennis players that Britain has produced. 'Bunny' Austin not only played in fourteen championships but for three years helped successfully to defend and hold the Davis Cup.

His rift with the All England Club was a purely family affair until Mr Austin made it all public in a book written by himself and his wife, Phyllis Konstam—*A Mixed Doubles* (Chatto and Windus).

This misunderstanding has stretched over eleven years since 'Bunny' Austin returned to England after the war and found that he was no longer a member of the club and had to re-apply for membership. He has now been waiting ten years for re-acceptance. He insinuates in his book that he has been discriminated against because of his association with Moral Re-Armament. He writes:

'The All England Club are entitled to do as they please. If they want to elect titled people; if they want to elect sons and daughters of committee members, and keep others on a waiting list for years, and if they do not want to re-elect me, it is their affair. But only to a point. The reason for rejecting an application for membership is important. If it is on account of a man's religious convictions it is dangerous. The very essence of sport and the hope

it offers to the world comes from the fact that it is above discrimination. Will we begin to apply this discrimination to Jews,
Catholics or those of different coloured skins? Where does it end?

'Whoever they are who want to keep me out of the All England
Club seem to be a powerful coterie and their power seems to
extend beyond the All England Club itself. For during the last
six years I have been in England, I have only been invited to one
lawn tennis function—to the fiftieth anniversary of the Frinton
Lawn Tennis Club.'

The All England's official reply is that Mr Austin, despite three
reminders sent him to America during the war, let his membership
expire. There is no deviation from the rules. Like everyone else,
he can re-apply and take his place on the membership waiting
list. As only five or six members are admitted yearly there is no
indication when his re-election comes up. The question of his
being involved with Moral Re-Armament simply does not come
into the question. Mr Austin claims he never received the letters.

'Bunny' Austin began his tennis career when he was five years
of age.

'At our home in South Norwood I used to watch my father
and one of his great friends, Mr A. D. Prebble, who played at
Wimbledon. Wimbledon became for me a magic name . . . a
tremendous dream. I started my tennis career by playing against
the nursery wall with my rocking horse as the net and one of my
chief opponents was the great lady champion, Mrs Lambert
Chambers.

'Why I chose a lady champion I am not quite sure. A few years
later I used to play with my sister Joan who was a natural tennis
player. We used to have terrific matches against each other and
my parents gave me permission to join the club, but at that stage
I never dreamed of playing anywhere except locally. Then my
father's Wimbledon friend said that my sister was good enough
to play in the junior championships and much to our amazement
and surprise, she won them. In the following week she went in
for the Surrey junior championships and my father suggested that
I might go into them with her and much to my surprise, and this

was one of the high peaks of my tennis career, I beat the reigning schoolboy champion. I was very small, only fourteen and he was seventeen. So that is how I was launched on my tennis career.'

Throughout his tennis days, 'Bunny' Austin had a hidden enemy—a sudden loss of energy, an overpowering weakness. Sometimes he would go out on to the court, easily win the first set and completely run out of energy unable to do anything about it for the rest of the game and be completely beaten.

'In those days I had no idea what this was due to. It made me very conscious of trying to keep up my health and eating the right food which was good. One year in the French championships I had no energy and could not even get from the service line to the net and was easily beaten. It was not until much later in my life when I was in the army in America and going through a physical check up that the medical officer noticed that I was jaundiced. It was then discovered that I had recurrent bouts of jaundice and this is a very rare complaint. At that time no one knew what caused it. Today they have discovered that it is a congenital defect of the liver and it strikes periodically.

'It is interesting to debate whether, in fact, if this had been discovered during my tennis days I would have been considered too great a physical risk for the Davis Cup.'

'Bunny' Austin was only nineteen when he was finally selected to play in the Davis Cup team. As secretary of the Cambridge University Lawn Tennis Club, he had already played in Germany where another member of the team was Kenneth Horne of the BBC. The university magazine, Granta, wrote that the name 'Bunny' was given Austin due to 'his quaint habit of consuming green food'.

'The truth is', says Austin, 'that at my school, Repton, they hit on "Bunny" because my second name was Wilfred and at that time there was a comic strip in which there were three characters, Pip, Squeak and Wilfred. Wilfred was a rabbit.'

'Bunny' Austin was in the team in 1933 when the Davis Cup returned to Britain after twenty-one years. France had held this cup for six years. Great Britain had won the final of the European zone of the Davis Cup from Australia which had been played on the Centre Court. Great Britain then went on to beat the United States in Paris in the inter-zone and finally won the cup from France in the Challenge Round by three matches to two.

On the first day, Fred Perry had beaten Cochet, and Austin had won from Merlin. But on the second day, Borotra and Brugnon, holders of the Wimbledon doubles title for the second year running, had beaten Harry Lee and Pat Hughes. The issue was decided on the final day when Cochet playing in his last Davis Cup for France beat Austin 5–7, 6–4, 4–6, 6–4, 6–4. The final match was between Perry and Merlin, the Englishman winning confidently over the nineteen-year-old Frenchman.

When France's defeat seemed certain, Borotra was said to have left the stand with tears in his eyes, saying:

'I can't watch this.'

At the end of the game, the frenzied French crowds showered cushions on to the court. It was 7.35pm when the 15,000 French, who packed the Stade Rolande Garros in Paris, stood to attention as the National Anthem was played.

There probably has never been a homecoming in tennis history quite like that. It deserves recording. As the Golden Arrow pulled into Victoria station at 8pm on 1 September, the sight of the Davis Cup in the window of the Pullman, with the melon-sized smile of the non-playing captain, H. Roper Barrett behind it, thousands of fans broke through the barriers and surged the door. Following the captain was 'Bunny' Austin, with the shield, with Harry Lee and Pat Hughes behind. Fred Perry who had saved the day was carried shoulder high.

Among those waiting to welcome the team was Suzanne Lenglen. At midday she had seen them leave Paris and later flown across to Croydon and driven to Victoria to greet them on arrival.

Twenty minutes after the train had arrived, the cup in its special sections was placed in a barrow with a few suitcases and wheeled away down the platform guarded by Mr Sabelli, secretary of the Lawn Tennis Association, and Mr Sterry, one of the vice-presidents.

The cup was classed as a 're-import' and no duty was paid on it.

'I am bound to ask you formally, Mr Barrett, whether you have anything in your possession which you have acquired abroad,' the customs officer said.

'Not a darned thing,' Barrett replied, holding the cup up.

At Dover the team had been greeted with a message of congratulations from the King. There was even a special dinner for the team at the Savoy Hotel arranged by the LTA. It was also the first time that the man in the street had taken lawn tennis to his heart in the same way as he did football, cricket and boxing.

'Bunny' Austin also made tennis history by being the first man to wear shorts at Wimbledon. He first wore them at Forest Hills in 1932. They were a sensation.

'Ah, you are prepared to wear them here but what about Wimbledon. Have you the guts?' his American friends asked.

'I first tried them out in Europe in the South of France. As I was leaving the hotel one morning wearing an overcoat over my bare legs, a young porter came up to me anxiously and said:

' "Excuse me, Mr Austin. I think you have forgotten your trousers." '

At Wimbledon that year, three other men players joined Austin.

'No explosion took place. The decorous stands at Wimbledon remained unshaken. No complaints were received from the committee. Shorts, as far as I was concerned, had come to stay.'

Today, 'Bunny' Austin has little time for tennis. As an official of the Moral Re-Armament's Westminster Theatre in London, this absorbs his whole life. He is still handsome in a suave way, and keeps up personal contact with many of the former Wimbledon champions.

No one thought in those early days that the marriage between a tempestuous movie and theatre star and the indulged tennis hero would last more than two years.

The Austins have now been married forty years and recently celebrated, with their son and daughter, their ruby anniversary.

'We have fooled the lot,' they say.

CHAPTER 12

Wimbledon at War

Mrs Rosie Cherry was sorting out the dresses and frilly
knickers in the 'Rabbit Warren' (ladies number 2 dressing-
room). Now in her seventies, like the swallows, she
returns every summer to Wimbledon where she has associations
going back forty-two years.

'Mum Cherry' the air force boys from the Dominions called
her. She was always there with her blunt humour, inimitable fruit
pies and prosaic approach to disasters, great or small.

The Royal Australian Air Force and the United States Forces
had an open invitation during the war to use the courts at Wimbledon as well as officers of the RAF.

Hugh Baker was one of them. From Sydney, he writes:

'Yes, Wimbledon brings back a lot of memories especially so
when the big tournament is again on over there. I was attached
to the ground staff in London and what with the extra daylight
during the summer we used to pop down to Wimbledon. A batch
of us would order sandwiches from the Boomerang Club at the
rear of Australia House which was run by voluntary help.

'Most of the chaps thoroughly enjoyed the privilege of using
the facilities at Wimbledon and playing on grass was quite a
novelty for some of the boys. Towards the end of the war we had
extra food allotted to us and any of our rations we would share
with Mum who was always so good to us.'

Mrs Cherry's eyes softened as she heard the letter and remembered how they would arrive with a handful of eggs expecting a miracle like the Lord and his fish.

'We had some really fine times. There was one of them, Dickie Mayer, we called "Hollow Legs". He could drink beer by the quart.'

The running of the All England Club during the war was due to the tenacity and dramatic vitality of the blonde personal assistant to the secretary, the late Norah Gordon Cleather. As a schoolgirl, her parents had taken her to the club in Worple Road. She was tennis-struck and remained that way all her life. Such is destiny that she finally reached Wimbledon in 1917, not as a player but via the games section of the Roehampton Club where she had worked.

Between the two wars she helped the secretary of the All England Club, Major Dudley Larcombe, and stayed there for twenty-five years. Formidable, capable, gregarious and collector of the famous, Norah Gordon Cleather loved her Wimbledon. In her book *Wimbledon Story* (Sporting Handbooks Ltd), she described that moment of history:

'I think it was when I first heard the metallic tramp of heavy feet in army boots marching along the Grand Walk outside the All England Club and echoing on the floor of the members' tea-room, that I really realised that Wimbledon had gone to war.

'When the 1939 championships came round, we ourselves had almost forgotten that we had such sinister signs of impending warfare on the very premises. Then, on 31 August, came the great reminder. That day the "crowd" moved in—nursing sisters, Red Cross and St John Ambulance personnel, ARP squads, doctors and the whole grim paraphernalia of Civil Defence.'

The members' tearoom became a canteen, so did the kitchens. The quiet reading-room with its old-fashioned air, its over-stuffed chairs and sofas, became a dormitory laced with prim iron bedsteads. The two big players' dressing-rooms and one of the small ones were turned into first aid posts. The treasurer's private office was a staff office.

One side of the premises was taken by the decontamination

Page 83
(*above*) That Wimbledon feeling—Mary Hardwick Hare
(former captain of the Wightman Cup), her husband
Charles (who played for the
Davis Cup) and Betty Nuthall
a Wimbledon star;
(*right*) two American darlings,
Maureen ('Little Mo') Connolly, champion 1952, 1953,
1954, and Doris Hart,
champion 1951

Page 84
(*above*) Elizabeth 'Bunny'
Ryan (USA), the greatest
doubles player in the
world, photographed in
1922. Her 'tennis im-
proved the day I gave up
wearing corsets';
(*left*) Helen Wills Moody
(USA) in a typical frozen
pose like a Greek frieze,
eight times winner of the
ladies' singles

authorities. The overseas boys arriving at the club used to bend double with laughter when they were greeted with the notice 'Remove all clothing except vest and knickers'.

The National Fire Service took up quarters round the number 2 court and in the vast rooms under the big stands by the electric score-board on number 1 court. Even the Army arrived in the shape of the London Irish who moved into the present Aorangi Sports Grounds which is owned by and adjoins the All England Club.

When the blitz began in earnest, Norah Cleather's own home was bombed out so she moved into residence in her small office and remained there for the duration.

As with the rest of England, food became monotonous and in short supply. Here she did a splendid job by installing a farmyard in one of the car parks.

'It was just like a real farm,' Mrs Cherry remembers. 'We had the lot—rabbits, chickens, ducks, geese, pigs and a donkey. There were cows in the other car parks and in another field there was a bull that used to upset our blackberrying for making pies.

'When a pig needed slaughtering, an SOS went out to Mr Higgins the family butcher at the top of the hill who still supplies the All England with its meat. Down he'd come and slaughter it in the boiler-house.'

The maintenance and ground staff were called up or volunteered until it was reduced from twenty to four. Indoors, Miss Cleather carried on with two stewardesses and one clerk until finally the clerk went and she was left to run the club alone.

On sunny, 'growing' days, she rounded up everyone for weeding. Down on their knees picking out any stray 'volunteers' (as they are called in groundman's parlance). The reward was a game of tennis. All the courts were used in rotation even the sacrosanct Centre Court.

Scattered round the Commonwealth now are some grey-haired veterans who can scarcely hold a tennis racket but are able to truthfully boast: 'When I played on the Centre Court . . .'

Wimbledon did not escape damage and has its typical blitz

F

stories. The first bombs had fallen on the competitors' stand in the Centre Court leaving an ugly wound. They had hit the gas mains and the shed where all the precious court equipment had been stored. Miss Cleather, Mrs Cherry, her son David and other members of the staff sheltering under the Centre Court miraculously escaped unhurt.

When the weather was fine, one of the toughest jobs the women did was unfurling the enormous canvas court covers to prevent them from rotting. Today it's a seven-a-side team of full-blooded students. In those days it was Norah, Rosie and anyone else they could drag in.

One of Miss Cleather's stand-bys was Ellis, an endearing relic from Victorian days. He treated visiting servicemen with a Jeeves-like devotion. After playing they were always greeted with his perfunctory inquiry:

'May I run a bath for you, sir, or will you take a shower?'

The Aussies loved it. These outsize bathtubs with long-handled scrub brushes and sponges as big as footballs are still in use today and treated with veneration by the visiting players.

During the V bombs play always continued until the engine shut off and then heads would go up to see in which direction it was going. The V2s were treated with contempt simply because they were not able to be heard or seen until they exploded.

During the two wars, Ellis had made himself one of the characters of Wimbledon. Dressed in a trim black coat, he would walk out behind the two players for the men's final carrying their rackets like the Crown Jewels.

Last year, diminutive Leo Turner of the number one dressing-room did it for the first time with immense dignity proving that it is not size but soul that matters in such Wimbledon ceremonial.

Ellis used to keep all the old blanket coats that his 'gentlemen' left behind in the lockers. When they died, he made them his personal property and ended up with a most illustrious collection.

When the war finished Colonel Duncan Macaulay, late of the 7th Gurkhas became secretary of the club and inherited Ellis who had known him when he was a young referee.

CHAPTER 13

The Post-War Scene

With the club's ration of whisky at one bottle a month, mowers that would not work, the back part of the club covered with broken glass from flying bombs, and no groundsman, the All England Club bravely decided early in 1946 that it must be business as usual and a tournament would be held that year.

A bold decision remembering that all the wartime restrictions were still in force. Everything was still rationed from food to soap, and tennis clothes and balls were almost non-existent. The greater part of the club premises were still in use by the various services and de-requisitioning permission had to be obtained.

The chairman, Sir Louis Greig, and the ex-Indian Army new secretary, Colonel Duncan Macaulay were determined. Unless the championships could be resurrected again there would be no money to help the Lawn Tennis Association, whose funds were perilously low, and tennis in general would have yet another set-back.

The bomb damage to the Centre Court was sealed off and with the help of the Mayor of Wimbledon, a great cleaning up campaign begun. The courts were cosseted back with re-sowing, rolling and mowing to their pre-war glory and reputation as the fastest grass courts in the world.

London was hungry for Wimbledon. The war had been won but this was a positive symbol that life was returning to normal. Seats were balloted for in the usual way in March, and the Services were advised that there were plenty of jobs going at Wimbledon as the normal ground staff had not yet returned.

Somehow and in some mysterious way the All England Club was ready for the first Wightman Cup which was played on 14 and 15 June, and when the tournament proper opened, even Queen Mary was back in the royal box.

In England, it had been a question of scratching together as many names as possible. Most of our top players had had very little or even no tennis during six years and were rusty. Mrs Menzies, the beautiful Kay Stammers, who had been runner-up to Alice Marble before the war and was a definite possibility for the championships, was now a mother of a family. The rest were Jean Bostock, Mary Halford, Mrs Passingham and Molly Lincoln. On the men's side, the hope was Tony Mottram, now twenty-six years old and desperately keen.

The American team was strong simply because they had had more facilities for practising during the war. The women looked like Amazons. They dressed alike, looked alike, spoke alike and played alike. There was Pauline Betz, Margaret Osborne, who later became du Pont, Louise Brough and Doris Hart. All coming to Wimbledon for the first time.

But they brought with them a new type of tennis—faster, more aggressive and an all-court game.

Among the American men was 'Big Jake' Kramer, just demobbed fighting fit from the United States Coastguards, and Tom Brown. France sent two players, both of whom had been prisoners of war, Yvon Petra and P. Pellizza. Geoff Brown and Dinny Pails played with the rugged individuality common to Australians. F. Pencec came from Yugoslavia, Jaroslav Drobny from Czechoslovakia and L. Bergelin from Sweden.

Among the men, Drobny and Kramer still return every year. Jack—as he is now called—Kramer's story is typical of the spirit of that year. Every year since 1960 he has covered 'The Fortnight' with Dan Maskell the ex-Wimbledon professional for BBC television. We spoke together in the BBC canteen, Kramer tucking into ham salad and a glass of milk. He has carried through to middle age all the charisma of the all-American boy that made him such a favourite in the forties.

On court he was the most favoured to win in 1946. Just twenty-five years old, tough and aggressive with an almost machine-like big-hitting game from both the backline and net. He also brought with him the grim determination of Tilden and Vines to win—and then reap the rewards as a professional.

'We all felt that we had to get back to Wimbledon. It was the greatest and if you won Wimbledon you had it all. During the war I was based in California half the time and on a ship in the Pacific for the rest. Actually it was the United States Coastguards, and I ended up in China which was pretty interesting. But no tennis. Wherever I went I took a racket with me but the only tennis I got was in the Admiralty Island Group when we went into dry dock.

'When I finally got permission to come over to Wimbledon it was as a member of the Davis Cup team and in those days this was far more important in the minds of players than it is today, which is a pity.

'Wimbledon is a pinnacle of sport. It is really marvellous the way this thing has been carried on through the years but now the money has made Wimbledon even more important than it used to be. In those days it was the great personal satisfaction that mattered. There was no prize money. You got a cup, no expenses and either your association sent you over or you sent yourself.

'I was an amateur and worked in a big sports company but I was only getting seventy-five dollars a week. My wife was pregnant but insisted on coming with me to Wimbledon. So we sold our car to dig up the money to pay for her and my association paid for me.

'In the days of the forties most of the money was given to players "under the table". It was against the rules to accept expenses, but to play tennis you had to have money.

'I remember it very clearly when we first arrived out here. The courts were awfully good—just terrific and I don't know how they got back into such shape in time. There was gaping bomb damage and it didn't look like today. But it was Wimbledon and we were here.

'I also remember the food was terrible—thin slices of meat with bread, potatoes and turnips. The American contingent stayed at the Rembrandt. I brought my own meat with me, two frozen tenderloins, which the local butcher kept for me in his freezer. If I wanted a steak for myself or a fellow player, I used to let him know and he'd bring them over. That poor pregnant wife didn't get any steak at all.'

In the human story of Wimbledon, Kramer's match with Drobny that year stands out as one of the most intense. As Kramer explained:

'In early 1946 I started training hard to make up for lost time and playing as much as I could. They changed the method of wrapping leather grips around rackets and I had a terrible case of blisters and it re-occurred on me twice. It bothered me at Queen's and I had to default, so when I got to Wimbledon the hand was still in a pretty bad shape. I took a lady's glove and played with the fingers cut off.

'Wearing the glove changed the feeling of the racket and I knew Drobny was a good player but I did not know that he was as good as he was. No one could predict form accurately that year. I finally had to get rid of the glove during the match as Drobny being a left-hander you always had to serve a lot of balls with slice to get the ball wide into his backhand. The glove put a lot of extra pressure on the fingers so before you know it you are getting blisters up in that area.

'The number one Dutch player at that time was also a doctor and he came out and during the change over doctored my fingers. Drobny won 6-3 in the first set but we had one set 18-16. I don't think in my entire life I had a loss that was more difficult for me than that one. But for the remainder of my tennis career this game at Wimbledon proved to be a source of strength because tennis is a game of feel and when you wear a glove on your hand and you have tape all over your fingers you lose a lot of your feel. But almost being able to beat Drobny, who was a damn tough tennis player, was fine. If in the future anything ever got rough on me out there I used to say to myself it can't ever be as tough as playing Drobny. It provided me with a mental clutch. After that I was able to win the doubles with Tom Brown.'

Jack Kramer is now associated with the Los Serranos Country Club just outside Los Angeles to the east towards Palm Springs area out in the citrus belt.

'I've been in this business on a silent partnership arrangement since 1952 when I was still playing and through my professional tennis promotion years. It's a public golf course with a private men's club and we have 150 of those golf chariots that people drive around and play golf in America now. When I got out of the tennis business I bought up all the shares and since 1961 I've been operating and owning it all.

'The BBC invited me to come over here in 1960 to do commentating. My wife says that my voice is much too high, and now I really don't feel that I add much. I thought at first that I had a lot of information of a different sort to Dan Maskell whom I am paired with and I could be completely different in voice and language. I have enjoyed it very much and been very proud to be with Dan Maskell. He's the greatest, he's a marvellous individual.

'When I first came here I used to get letters from people who disliked America and called me names and told me to go home. I even had a letter today from someone who was angry with me for mentioning Fred Perry and my friend 'Bunny' Austin. He felt that it was very improper of me to talk about those people who did nothing to help their country during the war. It is a great pity and has nothing to do with the Wimbledon spirit.'

The outcome of that first post-war Wimbledon was astonishing as both Drobny and Kramer were knocked out and the final was played between Yvon Petra who beat Geoff Brown.

Petra, tall and lanky, striding the court like Gulliver in Lilliput, was a fine showman as well as player. The crowds loved him. When he really meant business he put on his jockey cap, and they roared approval.

Kramer and Tom Brown won the men's doubles.

On the women's scene, it was an all-American show with the superb playing of Pauline Betz taking the title. Two women enjoyed special attention that year—Betty Nuthall of England and Doris Hart of America.

Betty ('Baby') Nuthall had first made headlines in 1920 when aged nine years wearing a Peter Pan collar on her schoolgirl dress, with long curls bouncing down her back, she had won the junior championships. She had arrived at Wimbledon aged fifteen, struggling through a difficult period when she was weighed down by a reputation too great for her to carry. Her fans expected her to sweep Wimbledon, but competitive international tennis is more demanding than that.

Now a mature player of thirty-five, she still had her following, and in her 1946 game she was matched against Mme Mathieu of France in the first round. The score was set all with Simone Mathieu leading 5-1 in the third set. Out came Betty's fighting spirit and finally she won 8-6. She won two more rounds before going down to Dodo Bundy of America, daughter of an early Wimbledon champion, May Sutton.

When Doris Hart took the court at her first Wimbledon she was greeted with a mixture of reverent admiration and curiosity. As a child she had been poisoned which had left her with a withered, mis-shapen right leg. No amount of skilful playing on her part could conceal the immense difficulties that she had to manoeuvre, but her own courage and the healthy robust attitude her family adopted, lifted her from the invalid class to world tennis. It was a stupendous act of courage only to be compared with Britain's Ann Haydon Jones who conquered a severe kidney disease and Alice Marble's victory over tuberculosis.

The Wimbledon crowds took to Doris Hart with the protective capacious love of a mother hen for its frailest chicken. She had just scraped into the team when Sarah Cooke dropped out. They noted and admired how by near perfect stroke playing she reserved her damaged leg. But it was not until five Wimbledons later in 1951 that she was on the Centre Court for a final. In just

over half an hour she won the title from her close friend Shirley
Fry, 6–0, 6–1.

Doris's win still ranks as one of the most popular finals ever at
Wimbledon. At the final ball given by the Lawn Tennis Association when the champions are required to make a speech, Doris
Hart's was one of the most poignant. Every champion reacts
differently. It is an immensely emotional time. Balancing between tears and sheer happiness, Doris Hart said she did not care
if she never won another tournament. She had won at Wimbledon.

Today she is still interested in tennis and carries on as a coach
for the Wightman Cup team, thus completing an inspiring tennis
career.

CHAPTER 14

Prestige Programmes

During 'The Fortnight' letters arrive at the All England Club's office asking for official programmes. There are orders from nearly every nation in the world where lawn tennis is played, as well as many of the overseas visitors to London who want to send a complete collection to friends back home.

At twenty new pence, they are considered by the general public as being 'a little expensive' but such is the quality of the production that the sales only cover the printing costs and profits come from advertising.

The programme as we know it today was the brain-child of Colonel Duncan Macaulay, who was then secretary.

'A friend who had been one of my officers during the war called to see me one day at Wimbledon when he was passing the club. He was a director of a firm of printers who also published and produced a well-known racing periodical called *Form at a Glance*. We got on to the subject of a programme for Wimbledon. I wanted a magazine that people would read and take away.

'I approached my old friend Sir John Smyth, the eminent tennis writer, and together we worked out the details.'

It began as a very simple programme in 1948 and then developed with an article every day and then a picture. Now it has a different colour and picture on the front page daily, an article written by Sir John Smyth appropriate to the events of that day, as well as three different pages of pictures of all the great players.

'There are six different colours for the Wimbledon programme each year,' producer Christopher Lampard explained. 'It takes weeks of study beforehand to choose colours that will sell well and are agreeable to the eye which is the whole object of the operation. The purple one is always for the Friday because this was the day when the Queen used to come.'

For a comparatively small firm the production has not always been easy. There was the printers' strike in 1959 just before the championship began.

'Suddenly I had to meet the committee—the same committee that decides everything—and explain to them that the programmes could not be produced. Most of the colour work in the region of 400,000 sheets were, in fact, printed. But how could we cope with the daily draw sheets?

'The committee decided to make a strong-arm gang and really by manpower force this paper out of the printing works on strike and take it elsewhere. Fortunately, we did not have to resort to this. I paid for the paper and printing involved, which ran into many, many thousands of pounds, and then subsequently moved it all with my own vans to various little printers and finishers throughout the suburbs of London who were not affected.'

The binding of the programmes had still to be achieved.

'We set up shop in one of the covered courts with my wife and a stitching machine. We were obviously being followed by the trade union fellows, fathers of the chapel, to see where we were getting this printing done—the daily draw sheets. It was all cloak and dagger stuff. I used to meet this particular fellow who was printing it in a pub in Wimbledon. My wife was the decoy. She would go into the pub and see him, the union fellow would follow her. They went out of one door and I then slipped out of another one. She would go off in my car and I would go off with the printer passing him the copy as we went.'

Tall, handsome and ineffably charming, Commander Lampard warmed to the tale:

'This worked very well until the middle Saturday. By then the buzz had got around. Someone did, in fact, trace us down to Clapham where the job was being done and got into the works, completely wrecking the machine. This was the only day that we failed to come out with the programme. It was the only time in the complete history of Wimbledon that we have failed our public. We managed to get going by the next week. It really was exciting —all these sheets arriving back into Wimbledon, being stowed in the covered courts and put together overnight with our own little stitching machine.'

Even today there are still crisis moments.

'Very often the referee cannot get an order of play until 9.30 or 10pm, particularly on the middle Saturday. This does make it difficult as Sunday is treble time which means that that particular programme is a costly exercise.'

Every morning about 11am the tall figure of Christopher Lampard is seen walking up and down the goods delivery entrance. The smart programme sellers are already waiting in their blue and white lollipop-striped booths. The minutes tick by. He frequently looks at his watch. Has the van broken down? At last it swings through the gate.

Christopher Lampard relaxes and allows himself a tot of pink gin . . .

Like everything else at Wimbledon, even the post office has an unworldly air about it. It stands—a Disney-like mobile van—just inside the gates on the right-hand side. In brilliant scarlet with its white and red awning, and tables and chairs for the public to sit and write their cards on. There is a special post box where for a little extra you can get your card marked 'Wimbledon Championships'.

For the first time in Wimbledon history, even the bank bent its rules last year and opened on the Sunday when heavy rain extended the championships for another day. Barclays Bank has a pretty blue and white banking chamber in the North Hall, and is ready for business from the time the gates open at noon. This year they may even install colour television where customers can sit and rest.

Time and time again one senses this extraordinary feeling of unreality about Wimbledon. You pinch yourself to see if it is all true—this bewitching blend of fantasy and fact, high professionalism and courtesy, the new world and the old.

CHAPTER 15

Five-Hour Drama

In the human history of Wimbledon one Olympian match stands out above all others. Ninety-three games of sweat, desperation, courage, pain and glory.

It was the great match in 1953 when thirty-one-year-old Jaroslav ('Old Drob') Drobny, that hard hitting, nuggety exile from Czechoslovakia, crashed over two cannon-ball services and two rocket-like drives to beat Budge Patty, Wimbledon champion of 1950.

The date was 26 June and the match began in blistering heat just after 4pm, and finished at 9pm. These five hours of drama had everything including two appeals against the light by bespectacled Drobny, which was unheard of before, and both players suffering from excrutiating pain through cramp. Drobny changed his glasses to pink lens reading ones when the light began to fade. Patty changed socks when his feet became blistered. Colonel Legg, the referee, had ruled that the game must go on.

Drobny finally won with a score 8–6, 16–18, 3–6, 8–6, 12–10.

Every year, Drobny still plays in the veterans' event and milling among the crowds he now looks more like a respectable solicitor's clerk than the persistent tennis player that he was. It was not only his dogged determination that endeared him to the crowds but his humanity and fine sportsmanship.

Just a few months before Wimbledon opened last year Jaroslav

Drobny fulfilled a dream. He opened his own spankingly modern sports shop in London's South Kensington and it was here that I found him amid packing cases.

As he talked aloud to himself remembering back to that sizzling day nineteen years ago, I had the distinct feeling that he had forgotten I was there at all. His voice, quiet and heavily accented rolled on:

'It was 4.15pm and Budge Patty and I knew that we were going to stay on court at least two hours because we always had a tough match. On grass this is not such a long time and it is not easy to break anybody's good serve on grass and we knew it.

'At 6.15pm we were only one set all. You don't look at time, you don't feel physically exhausted because after all anyone playing at Wimbledon trains to last for three hours at least. Once we go over three hours it is not the physical strain but the mental one. People watching might see you slow down a little but you yourself are not conscious of this because your opponent does exactly the same thing.

'It is the mental strain. You suddenly think to yourself that one shot against you puts you out of the championship and it means you have to wait another year. The mental strain is something which nobody can train for.

'You get disturbed, frightened, you argue to yourself, shall I take a risk or should I play safe and so on? In those few seconds from when your opponent serves so many things go on in your mind. This is how you get mentally exhausted.

'The mental approach to the game at Wimbledon is more than in any other tournament because every tennis player in the world wants to win there. It is the best tournament in the world. If you win it you are considered the best player in the world. Once you win Wimbledon you don't have to win any other tournament that year. To be single-handed champion of the world is what every player is fighting for.

'Back to my match with Patty. I had won the fourth set so I am relieved and Patty gets a little bit mentally disturbed because we are now equal again and when it comes to the fifth set anything

can happen. And it did because again he had match point before
he finally lost. The tennis was of a very high quality even now
which was surprising as before we had had exciting matches but
never one like this. But on that particular night we played above
our form—we were able to check this by seeing it on a film later
on.

'My wife who was watching the match, and friends were also
mentally exhausted but just imagine what it is like to be the
player—the agony and so on. And then the most dramatic moment
of all came. He was leading 5-4 and here I was just about to
serve when suddenly I got cramps, real cramps for the first time
in my life. It was in my thigh and I just didn't know what to do.
I had seen it with other people but here suddenly I was confronted
with it myself.'

The heat of the afternoon and tension was so great at this point
that people in the crowd were actually fainting while on court
Drobny writhed with pain.

'Suddenly I remember my good friend Ted Schroeder who beat
me in a final in 1949 and got the title. I remember that I have
seen him, not at Wimbledon but somewhere else, when he got
cramps. It had stayed in my mind—what did he do? I remembered.
He walked up and down to try and shake it off. Incredible as it
may seem but at that particular moment when I was struggling
with this terrific pain I could not lift my leg at all. I could not
even move it. It was as if it was paralysed. Somehow I got myself
going and so managed to shake it off.

'I was just about to serve and when I looked up to see if my
opponent was ready I see he is on the ground. He is in agony. He
has got the cramps too. So here we are both struck with the cramps
at the same time. It was an incredible feeling. It's very difficult
to describe but we both just wanted to get the game over because
we were physically so exhausted not really knowing anything. We
did not know if we had played three, four or five hours. Our
minds were muddled. You just have to go on playing. It is when
you read about it later or somebody tells you that you broke this
or that record that you are conscious of it. But at that moment on

the court you just keep on and on. You win your serve. He wins
his. You go on and on. It is the sheer guts that gets you through.
This cramps is something I will never forget as long as I live.

'When I looked up and saw Patty in the same agony I think
this was the moment that got me through, the moment that lifted
me up again. I thought:

' "Well, if he is as bad as I am then there is nothing between us."
I go on and somehow we both managed to shake it off. Cramps
is a thing which is not continuous, it stays a while, then goes and
then comes back again. You feel your muscles getting tighter and
tighter, and then you start moving quicker to control it and somehow you manage. You play one point and you may win it against
the cramps, against your opponent and so on, and I think this is
more than people watching actually realise.'

Drobny had not eaten since breakfast except the sugar lumps
which he sucked between games instead of the usual salt. Suddenly
the marathon ends with a stinging return by Drobny. They both
reach the side of the court and sportsman that he is Drobny
put his arms round Patty. At that moment they were both
oblivious of the thunderous applause.

'I felt like an actor who was ill and takes the stage just the
same. I hated disappointing the crowds. They seemed somehow
to have taken me to their hearts,' Drobny told reporters after the
match.

Looking back now, he remarks:

'We did not collapse like some other people. We both had
managed to finish with our feet up but the moment we hit the
dressing-room I can assure you that we both collapsed again with
terrible pain because once you sit down and sort of relax that is
the worst thing.

'Again I tried to remember what to do. Someone had told me a
long time before that hot baths were a good thing against the
cramps. So I jump into the bath—they have such beautiful tubs
at Wimbledon. I just did not care if I had won or lost at that
moment I was in such terrible pain, and so was my friend Patty.
Suddenly I shriek like hell because at that particular moment I

G

got the cramps all over my body—every muscle was searing pain. I can't describe it but it is as if someone takes a knife and starts carving you alive. The pain is absolutely ridiculous. People rushed round me and fished me out. They tell you that you shouldn't have got into the bath but by then it is too late.'

Drobny never had an attack of cramp again in his life, although he did play in several other long matches. His deduction today is that it was the mental strain that brought the cramp on.

'I talked to Patty afterwards and we both agreed that it was not the length of the game but the strain. I had played on hard courts for three and a half or four hours before, and on hard courts you run twice as much as you do on grass. But I had never felt so exhausted before. Patty had had three match points in the fourth set and another three in the fifth.'

The score card of this great match was photographed and is kept framed in the All England Club and both players were presented with silver cigarette cases by the late Duchess of Kent.

Though no one could visualise Drobny and Patty being in any condition to play for some time, they did team up next day in a doubles match. Patty, the sinewy bean pole, recovered physically quicker than Drobny and only the greatest guts got this tough sportsman through until he was beaten by Kurt Nielsen of Denmark. He had gone further than any other Scandinavian and was the first unseeded player for twenty-three years to have reached the finals.

'Old Drob', the 'Old Warhorse', as he was affectionately called, took fifteen years and eleven attempts before he finally became Wimbledon champion in 1954. With the whole of the Centre Court charged with sympathy and passion for this great player who has played tennis under three flags—his own country, Egypt and now Great Britain—he defeated the young Australian Ken Rosewall. The match lasted two hours and thirty-five minutes with a final score of 13–11, 4–6, 6–2, 9–7.

It also proved what a game and courageous fighter Rosewall was who went on to the court knowing that everyone hoped it would be victory for Drobny. As one sportswriter said:

'Sometimes when this game Sydney kid served an unpopular point, it sounded as though only his mother were in the stands, so solitary was the clapping.'

It was Jaroslav Drobny more than any other player who influenced the bringing about of the open championship. Drobny without a country, under no control from any association, able to lap up the money with his popularity and great play.

Today Drobny still remains one of the Wimbledon legends.

'People used to say about me that I was a nervous player. Well, it's true, I was. I showed it with my emotions. But any other players like Patty or now last year Stan Smith, they are just as nervous, with the exception that they don't show it as much. They have the same butterflies. They go to the toilet many times before a match like everyone else. It is just a question of how you show it.

'I remember my great friend Borotra. You have never seen him get upset. He had that nice smile no matter what, but I can assure you that I have seen him upset many, many times but because of that smile even in the moments when he was angry and fighting to control himself, he was able to hide it.

'You see others like Nastase just lets it be known that he's upset. That is why the people like him. It is the human element. That is why perhaps I was liked because I was a human being and people could identify themselves with me. I used to get mad, Gonzales would get mad but at ourselves. Not like some of the youngsters today who get mad at the linesman, the umpire, their opponents and so on, which is completely wrong. How can I murder the fellow because he makes a very good passing shot? This is what is happening today. It's very wrong. I have seen people being passed at the net—'That's a good shot,' we used to say. 'You lucky so and so.' But they don't do that now.

'A very great friend of mine is Peter Ustinov who is also a great tennis fan. I have asked him many, many times are you nervous after so many years when you go to make a speech or joke, and he says:

' "I'm more nervous now than I used to be. I am always nervous, because if you are not before the performance it means that you are no good."

'And this is true. The tennis player is really an actor on the court. Then you have people like Smith who can control himself. Perhaps control is the wrong word for that is the way he is. Smith is a temperamental fellow. We all are because the strain is very big but Smith is made that he doesn't show it.

'The Wimbledon crowds are very funny and very sensitive. They can tell if you are misbehaving on purpose, if you are deliberately trying to upset someone or if you do it because that is the way you feel. That is the difference.

'People like myself. I'd rather go and watch Gonzales any time than watch anybody else because he thrills me with this emotion. We had the little Maureen Connolly. She hardly smiled. She kept to herself her emotions and that is why perhaps the public never really took her up like some other champions who were not as good as she was because she was certainly one of the greatest. And today we have Evert. She is loved and admired, she is seventeen and she's a beautiful girl. If she was just a little bit older and if she had not had such fantastic publicity before she made her first Wimbledon, people would not have taken her up as big as they did. I'm not trying to pull her down but merely explain how the Wimbledon public react to certain people.

'Goolagong is a little bit too happy-go-lucky, nevertheless the people love her because she laughs. Chris Evert is very lucky because she's a great tennis player, she will probably overcome the strong face which she has now and start smiling a little bit. I hope she does.

'Billie Jean King, unfortunately, never got the imagination of the Wimbledon people from the start. Just when she was about to become a good player and great champion she used to shriek at every point. She opened her mouth all the time. She talked and talked and never stopped. She was smiling but it wasn't a humorous laugh. One could see that it was sarcastic—it was a laugh which sort of says ha! ha! ha!—and people reacted to it. Certainly she started the wrong way and will never get the Wimbledon public back. They will always be against her and she will never be acclaimed a great champion in such a way as she really deserves.'

We talked too of the prize money today, which Drobny thinks is stupidly high.

'As far as I am concerned they are all paid like queens and kings. Not one of them deserves as much money as they are making. Nobody can tell me that a fellow like Laver, or whoever it is, can make £5,000 or dollars in one match. There is not the slightest doubt in my mind that they are over-paid. It is thanks to sponsors that they get this money, but I am always counting on the people they attract to watch them, the same as an actor. If you think of the great scientists and doctors and diplomats what they earn a year and then what these tennis players are getting paid a week for doing what is fun to them anyway. It is ridiculous. They deserve to be paid obviously because they are entertainers but not these exaggerated prices. I am sure that some day it will level itself up.

'Right now there is a very big boom in tennis and sponsors are just lavishing money right, left and centre. But it's going to stop as it stopped in many other sports before. Present tennis players are very lucky because they can make a lot of money and good luck to them but it won't last unless you can find players like Gonzales, Santana, Sedgman, Cochet to bring the public back. Unless the tennis tournaments in the world can do this people would rather sit at home and watch it on television, which is wrong. You have to get the public there where they see the game played in the flesh and the youngsters will then take it up. But just watching tennis on television this does not improve tennis in general. And this is why Wimbledon has more chance to survive than any other tournament. It has a human relationship with its players.'

Patty now lives in Switzerland where he is in the real estate business in Lausanne. Still tremendously fit with a body that has worn well, he comes back every year to Wimbledon. His competitive tennis days are over for the moment.

'I haven't played much tennis recently because I hurt my back about a year ago, and jumping round the courts sort of aggravates it. I'm forty-eight now and I would have played in the veterans this year, but I don't dare play.'

During the war Patty was a private in the Army stationed in Europe for three years. He liked the atmosphere of cluttered Europe and with his little savings, settled in Switzerland.

His summing-up of Wimbledon reflects the opinion of most of the older champions.

'The quality of tennis at Wimbledon in general is better than in my day. If you were one of the top seeded players we used to have it rather easy in the first two or three rounds but now even that first round is difficult as there are so many good players. In general there are so many more good players now so, of course, the standard is much higher.'

CHAPTER 16

The Royal Family at Wimbledon

There has always been an umbilical tie between the British Royal Family and Wimbledon. It dates back to 1919 when King George V and Queen Mary first went to watch the tennis at the old Worple Road grounds. They had been persuaded to lend their patronage by the club secretary, Commander George Hillyard, who had served on the royal yacht *Britannia* and was a close friend of the King.

He shrewdly realised the value of the mystique surrounding the First Family which mesmerised the British public. The arrival of King George V and Queen Mary was the final accolade needed to raise the All England Club to the fashionable grandeur of Ascot, Henley and Cowes.

It was therefore perfectly natural that when the new Wimbledon grounds were opened in Church Road that the King and Queen were present as well as the Prince of Wales and Princess Mary. By now they were 'hooked' on tennis, having watched those giants Suzanne Lenglen, 'Big Bill' Tilden, 'Jo' Anderson, Gerald Patterson and Borotra. These were the great flowering years for the All England Club and a whole new rebirth in the interest of tennis.

From then on until she died—twenty-nine years later—Queen Mary made Wimbledon a special part of her summer season. She really cared for tennis. The combination of an immaculate green court, players in stark white and the self-discipline involved, appealed to her fastidious nature. Even when she was in her eighties and the last match went on late, she insisted on remaining until the end. A message would be telephoned to Marlborough House to say 'Dinner will be late'.

For twenty-four years Miss Ruby Harris was the 'royal waitress' and every year brought its own special reunion with Queen Mary. Miss Harris retired two years ago but over our own special coffee party we talked about that astonishing woman.

Every year Queen Mary used to take tea in the special 'royal room', which during the rest of the year is used as a small dining-room for club members. Its Englishness is heartful—white wicker furniture, pastel walls and glorious chintz curtains. On the Queen entering the room, Ruby, wearing her black uniform and spanking white apron and cap, would step forward. It was always the same routine.

'Now, my little friend,' Queen Mary would say. 'Here are three things—my umbrella, my programme and my scarf. Take care of them for me, please.'

Queen Mary then settled herself at the round table, with its special Irish lace cloth which is still used, her back to the wall and facing the entrance. She wanted to see everything that was going on. Every year her tea was the same—brown bread and butter with bramble jelly, tomato bridge rolls and chocolate cake. After anything sweet she always finished up with a slice of plain bread and butter. Both King George and Queen Mary drank China tea which they brought with them in an Oxo box which was duly placed on the kitchen shelf and the remains taken back to Buckingham Palace when they left.

In those days the royal box always had raspberries as well as the traditional strawberries. Queen Mary always requested:

'I'll have a little bit of both, thank you.'

Ruby still blushes when she remembers the day when Queen Mary stood up ready to leave.

'I first handed her the umbrella without which she would not move. In my hand I had what is called in our profession a rubber.

It is a square of linen—immaculate and white, folded into eights. Change it every five minutes if you wish but it must always be spotless. Queen Mary as usual began asking me questions as to whether I had seen the tennis and so on as I handed her the three things. She saw the rubber, took it and put it round her neck. My expression must have been awful.

' "Your Majesty," I said. "Oh, ma'am, I am so sorry but you have my rubber that I use for wiping things. This is your silk scarf."

'She looked at me for a few seconds and a huge grin came across her face. She then continued:

' "Now how many years have we been together there?"

'Still flustered, I counted up and said, "Seven."

' "No, eight years," she replied immediately. Her memory was fantastic and, of course, she was right. She then took me to see the prints on the wall of the members' sitting-room. There was one favourite of hers—two players on an immaculate tennis lawn looking at a daisy of all things.

' "What about that," she said triumphantly.

'I had seen it before and replied: "Isn't it wonderful."

' "Beautiful, beautiful," she murmured.

'In that moment Queen Mary was speaking to me as a friend. The awkwardness of the rubber incident was firmly forgotten. No wonder we all adored her.'

Everyone at the All England has his or her Queen Mary story. Their eyes mist over and they get a far-away intonation in their voice and then press you to listen. Some are not worth recording they are so slight but they are a measure of the veneration she inspired.

Queen Mary had the habit of moving back in the royal box as the sun got lower in the western skies at the end of the day. As the American champion Vic Seixas explained:

'Of course every time she would get up to move back everybody would stop and stand, thinking that she might be leaving. She'd get up, pick up her umbrella, walk back a row and then sit down again. It took a minute or so. One afternoon I was playing, she did it three or four times. It was very funny and disquieting, but she was so knowledgeable about the game that she knew exactly when to cause the least interruption. The players never minded.'

This particular evening the match went on much longer than normal which meant that Queen Mary made many moves. In the end she arrived at the back row which was desperately unsafe should the back legs of the chair tipple back. Colonel Macaulay, the secretary, spotted the danger and immediately took up a crouching position behind to bolster up the back of the Queen's chair.

Queen Mary was totally unaware of the situation as she watched the tennis.

'Colonel Macaulay, I do hope that you can see. You seem rather low down there,' she inquired, without turning round.

In fact, Duncan Macaulay was stiff with cramp and sat there scared to move or sneeze until the final of the game.

When it was known in 1951 that Queen Mary, who was then eighty-three, might have difficulty in managing the steps up to the royal box, a special sedan chair was prepared. The Queen was advised and replied that she would be grateful to use it as long as the public did not see her getting into it or getting out. In order to test the whole operation, Lady Greig, wife of the chairman, acted as royal 'stand in' just before 'The Fortnight' with half a dozen strong sailors doing the carrying. Over and over again they rehearsed until the chair just floated up.

Queen Mary's health deteriorated and she decided not to go to Wimbledon that year because of the intense heat. She died just before 'The Fortnight' began. The chair was sadly banished to the cellars where it remains to this day.

During the Wimbledon season, the royal family has its own retiring room. It is a pretty room in soft pastel tones with chintz, washbasin and dressing-table much in the style of the Ritz Hotel. But the lavatory has always produced its own dramas. There was the day, for instance, when Princess Marie Louise found the delphiniums there. The flowers from the royal rooms are changed every day during the tournament and divided among the staff attending the rooms. One of the women cleaners had been given delphiniums and decided the royal lavatory pan was just the place to keep them fresh and cool. During the afternoon there was a shriek from Princess Marie Louise who had retired:

'Take those things out of there immediately.'

The delphiniums were removed in a matter of seconds.

King George V also had some difficulty with the same small room. He got locked in. Mrs Rosie Cherry who now looks after one of the women players' dressing-rooms during the championships, was known for her strength and quick thinking. An SOS was sent for Rosie who took matters into her own hands immediately.

'Stand back, your Majesty—I'm pushing it in,' she cried, and then putting her shoulder to the door, crashed triumphantly through.

'The King looked a little startled,' she told me with an impish grin. 'But the thing was to act quickly.'

It has been customary for some years for the President of the Club to attend a luncheon party before the Final of the men's singles and this is now held in the Members' Enclosure. On one occasion when the Queen accepted an invitation it was held in the club house. As there was a heatwave at the time large blocks of ice were placed in front of electric fans.

If this seems strangely out of date in this age of astronauts and advanced science no one minds. It contributes as much to the ambiance as the white wicker tables and chairs, and salad Wimbledon—a red apple hollowed out and filled with chopped apple, nuts, cream and mayonnaise.

During Princess Marina's term of office, ten minutes before she left, a member of the catering staff would slip out and place two boxes on the front seat of her car. They contained two chocolate gateaux and two bars of chocolate. The cake, specially made for Wimbledon, is unbelievably good, peat brown and moist with ground almonds in the mixture. One was for Princess Marina and the other for her chauffeur.

Princess Marina's association with Wimbledon lasted for

twenty-five years. It was an affair of the heart between this practically all-male bastion and an extremely beautiful woman. Also they had one thing in common—tennis.

When the Duke of Kent was killed in an air crash in 1941, it was decided after a committee meeting to ask the Duchess to take over the position of president of the All England Club, and this she did until her death in 1968. She loved her Wimbledon and had the consoling ability of making everyone at their ease.

At the top of the stairs to the members' lounge is an arresting portrait of her by the Hungarian painter Judy Cassab. Painted in glowing colours—citron yellow, orange fizz with a touch of flamingo, the eyes are gentle, the smile indecisive and the beauty magnetic. Time after time I have watched members pass it and look up. A shy smile appears on their faces as if they were pleased she was still at Wimbledon.

Princess Marina had always loved tennis. On her marriage she had a hard court laid at 'Coppins', the Kent's home at Iver, and she was the fastest player in the family. She encouraged all her children to play tennis and although racing cars take first place in the present Duke of Kent's life he, too, has inherited her interest in tennis.

'She looked on Wimbledon as a holiday,' Herman David told me. 'She did not like to have official guests. She always used to say: "Are they going to talk?" '

Chatterboxes were sent to the back of the royal box so that she could get on with the serious business of watching the tennis. She knew all the players by their names and just before Wimbledon would invite the secretary to lunch to brief her on the newcomers. Manuel Santana of Spain was a special favourite and she never missed seeing him play.

When Herman David was first made chairman in 1959, he was nervous as most sincere Englishmen are on meeting a member of their royal family for the first time.

'I stood waiting trembling at the door with my wife. As we were going up the staircase into the Centre Court, Princess Marina looked over the top and saw two champions playing. She turned to me and said: "Those two look rather nervous, don't they?"

'I said: "Yes, ma'am, especially the one who is playing the champion because after all he has never played on the Centre Court before."

'She waited a minute and suddenly turned to me and said:
' "Are you nervous?"

'I said: "Yes, ma'am—to tell you the truth. Very nervous."

' "Never mind," she said. "We will be getting on like a house on fire in twenty-four hours." '

It was Princess Marina who inspired boiled sweets in the box. Along with the infra-red heaters and foot-high troughs of hydrangeas there are now two chintz-covered waste-paper baskets of boiled sweets. After a particularly long rally one day, Princess Marina said:

'We could do with some sweets in these long rallies.'

Now every morning Mrs Herman David selects the day's quota. To the service staff manning the box they are known as 'the royal nutties' (a naval term for lollies). Just before the royal party is due to arrive plain clothes detectives frisk the nutty baskets in case of hidden bombs.

There was nothing stuffy about Princess Marina at Wimbledon. Surrounded by her club members, who frankly adore her, she bloomed as any woman would. The fashions too amused her. When 'Gorgeous Gussy' wore her lace panties, the Princess was the first to tell Duncan Macaulay that she liked them and they were fun.

Princess Marina was always quick to spot the fashion surprises. When one player walked on to court number 1 one year Herman David remarked to Princess Marina:

'Look, ma'am. She's got purple pants on.'

'She's got green on. I am so certain that I'll bet you that.'

'Ma'am, you'll lose,' the chairman replied.

'Never mind. We'll have half a crown on it.'

When the player came round to the royal box end and served, to everyone's delight, one half of her panties was green, the other half purple.

'Good heavens,' gasped Princess Marina. 'What a funny place to wear the club colours.'

Princess Alexandra always manages to fit in at least one day at Wimbledon each year. When she first went after Princess Marina died, she turned to Herman David and said:

'My mother's ghost walks here.'

And that is exactly how the All England Club wishes it.

Although the Queen is patron of the club, she has only visited Wimbledon twice during her reign—in 1957 and 1962. As everyone clearly knows, horses and not tennis are her interest. On one of her visits during 'The Fortnight', Prince Philip slipped quietly out of the royal box when he had had enough tennis and settled himself in front of the television in the members' sitting-room watching the test match. One of the elderly club members noticing this and not recognising him, was piqued and remarked tartly:

'Young man, you are sitting in my chair.'

'Sorry, sir,' the Duke said, and quickly moved.

On occasions when the test cricket and Wimbledon overlap, the members have a cunning way of switching the television over to cricket when no one is looking.

Although she does not play herself, the Queen has done much to encourage her children in tennis. Dan Maskell went regularly to Buckingham Palace to coach Princess Anne and Prince Charles when they were younger.

'Had she applied herself with the same dedication to tennis as she does to horse riding, there is no doubt that Princess Anne could have become a really fine player at championship level. She is an absolute natural with disciplined movements and a quick eye. It is marvellous to watch her well-trained brain and how quickly she grasps anything.'

The late King George VI is the only member of the royal family to have actually played at Wimbledon. It was in 1926 when he won the RAF doubles with Wing-Commander Sir Louis Greig, thus enabling him to qualify for the Wimbledon championships. At the time Sir Louis lived in Thatched Cottage, now the home of

Princess Alexandra and Mr Angus Ogilvy on the edge of Rich-mond Park. Prince Albert, his brothers Prince George and Prince Henry were frequent visitors. As Lady Buchan Hepburn, the former Bridget Greig, remembers:

'We used to have marvellous Sunday afternoon parties at my parents' home. All three of the Princes used to come there for weekends. They joined in with everything like bathing the children and family tennis. Helen Wills, Helen Jacobs and Von Cramm often came too, but they all played like professionals and had never heard of English "Sunday tennis".'

Prince Albert played left-handed and was very competent, but Louis Greig never was inclined to position himself so that his royal partner could put up a good show. When they played at Wimbledon on the number 2 court, watched by the Queen Mother, they were quickly defeated in straight sets by that long experienced pair of former champions A. W. Gore and H. Roper Barrett.

After his succession to the throne, King George VI did not play in public again.

CHAPTER 17

The Royal Box

During 'The Fortnight' the most hallowed piece of ground apart from the turf of the Centre Court is the royal box, perched on the south side of the arena.

Here, apart from club officials, sit members of the royal family, and 900 distinguished guests who have been invited by the committee of twelve members. They are selected in batches of seventy a day. For the rest, the invitation is treated with the reverence due to such a luxurious perk amid the summer social round.

Several weeks before the championships the guests receive a letter from the secretary inviting him or her, with an extra seat, for such and such a day, and such is the prestige of these invitations that ex-ambassadors have been known to pale when they realised that they were no longer on the 'list'.

'If we don't like them or their behaviour, they are not asked again,' Herman David explained. And you know it's true.

Guests to the royal box are expected to reply well in advance, but members of the royal family and cabinet ministers are accommodated within an hour's warning.

For the last seventeen years, Sir George Titman, aged eighty-three, has had the awesome task of arranging each morning the seating in the box.

There are the two faces of Sir George. The poker one that befits the former secretary to the Lord Chamberlain's office and author of *Dress and Insignia Worn at Court*. Distinguished, discreet, keeper of the Queen's secrets . . .

His eyes avert when I inquire about his own orders.

'Oh, well, there is the CBE and MVO and about six various foreign orders which I picked up during my rather long time in the Royal Chamberlain's office.'

Each morning, Sir George arrives at noon at the secretary's office and collects his list. There are about seventy names each day to be juggled and placed in correct order. In former years the lists tended to be drawn from royal circles, diplomats and government officials. Now they embrace a cross-section of the public life of this country. A well-known TV personality or actress can find herself happily sitting next to a racing driver. A headmistress from a girls' school chats to a cabinet minister.

Last year, Sir Brian Horrocks sat in front of the headmaster of Eton, and Yehudi Menuhin was placed in the row ahead of Lord Rupert Nevill. At tea time, Peter Ustinov found himself engrossed in tennis talk with the Duchess of Kent, while the Duke of Kent made a beeline for the racing driver Jackie Stewart, and boxing champion Henry Cooper.

When Miss Ginger Rogers was on a visit to London some years ago, she was invited to the royal box. She shone like the one gold-papered chocolate in a box of plain. A friend from Texas noticed her and bulldozed his way to the entrance hoping to speak to her. After minutes of arguing and cajoling, a note with his name was discreetly slipped to her.

Later the Texan was to say:

'Oh, boy. Getting into that box was worse than Fort Knox.'

When I asked Sir George how he coped with the seating of ambassadors from unfriendly countries, he looked at me reprovingly:

'Ambassadors are always placed in strict precedence so that there is no question of whether they are friendly or not. It doesn't matter. They know their own precedence by the date that they are accredited to the Court of St James.'

At the request of the Foreign Office, visiting royalty from abroad are always accommodated at Wimbledon, often at very short notice. One afternoon in recent years at 5pm the Foreign

H

Office rang to say that a king from an African state would be arriving at the club in an hour's time.

An appropriate chit was passed to Herman David who was sitting in the front row, who then arranged suitable accommodation in the box. The king arrived with several members of his staff all colourfully and appropriately dressed. After an hour of watching the king indicated that he would like to leave but wondered if he could have a drink while waiting for his car. He retired into the members' dressing-room and his aide took up position outside the door with hand never far from the dagger.

The king reappeared, had his drink and stepped down to the Rolls-Royce supplied by the Foreign Office.

The chairman wished him good-bye and hoped that he had had an enjoyable afternoon.

'I have thoroughly enjoyed myself at Henley,' the king replied.

The security arrangements in the royal box are naturally tight. Plain clothes police mingle with the mighty and the back row of the box is reserved for private detectives on duty.

When Patricia Nixon, daughter of Richard Nixon, President of the United States, visited Wimbledon she arrived with two private detectives who asked to be seated near her. Officials were nonplussed.

'Why two?' they asked. 'We have royalty every day and we've never lost one yet.'

By tradition the royal box is staffed by the Services. Since 1964, Warrant Officer George Eldridge has been in charge. Like all the other service people at Wimbledon, he arranges his holidays so that they fall during 'The Fortnight'.

'I wouldn't miss it for worlds,' he told me. 'Where else could I meet all these distinguished people who greet me year after year. Names like Bing Crosby, Charlton Heston, Sir Stanley Matthews, Mrs Odette Hallowes, Enoch Powell, Lady Spencer Churchill, Hayley Mills.'

Warrant Officer Eldridge's eyes misted as he remembered back over the years.

'There was Mr Attlee—he used to come year after year. In the end we used to practically carry him into his seat and wrap him up in a rug. Just a featherweight.'

The Prime Minister who gave India her independence, was by then so small, so frail like a London sparrow. When it was time to leave he would perk up and thank everyone for 'such a lovely day of tennis'.

Whenever the television cameras panned on to the royal box, you could see Warrant Officer Eldridge standing at the entrance to the box having a quiet chew. He is a man who relies on his gum during such concentrated duties.

Back at the mess in High Wycombe he used to come in for some gentle après-Wimbledon ribbing.

'You're third in the ratings after *The Man from Uncle* and *Coronation Street*.'

This year, Eldridge retires from the Air Force and unless a miracle happens, he will be watching on his television—mentally checking 'The Box', noting his successor and wishing that time had stood still.

The magnetism of Wimbledon is strong and imperishable to its loyal servants.

One person who would have loved to have been admitted to the royal box was Lady Dorothy Paget, one of the richest women in England. With her lady companion she wanted to take her picnic into the Members' Enclosure but was barred simply because she was not a member.

She stormed and protested and finally swept her large body and basket into one of the public lavatories muttering:

'I am Dorothy Paget.'

With great deliberation she shut the door, locked it and posted her companion outside. She then set her picnic out on the floor.

No one, but no one could move her. She was enjoying her champagne immensely.

Long after the last set had been played Lady Dorothy was still picnicking. The door was still locked.

Colonel Macaulay, the secretary of the All England Club, was informed. In his most charming and persuasive manner he talked to her through the door. There was no response only the clink of a glass against a bottle and a pleasant gurgle-gurgle sound.

A great calm descended. It had been a good picnic and Lady Dorothy was tired. She wanted to sleep. Her companion stood outside the locked door like a faithful dog tolerant of its mistress's whims.

'Very well,' urged the colonel. 'There is only one thing I can do now. I will lock you in this part of the building. We will return in the morning to let you out.'

Slowly the key was turned. Lady Dorothy went home.

CHAPTER 18

The Americans in the Fifties

You can spot those American veterans of the fifties at the Wimbledon tournament. There is something special about them—lean giants, amazingly preserved, suntanned, with faces that time has embalmed. No one has worked harder on keeping young mentally and physically.

Weaving among the players last year was Vic Seixas and his southern belle Dolly. In the fifties when Dolly arrived, the transport staff of the All England Club always tried to arrange that the Seixases had their own car. Nothing to do with Helen Wills Moody's Garbo act but merely because Dolly's New Look dresses must not be crushed. She sat in the back with her petticoats frothing and foaming around her like an advertisement for detergents. She was beautiful then and now, on the opening day, in her pristine white pleated skirt, blazer, white cotton gloves and shining black hair swept up into a French twist, she was the most elegant woman at the tournament. Every day Dolly changed her outfit and ribbon bow pinned at the back of her head. She has that special American look with trim, slim legs and feet, similar to the Duchess of Windsor.

'You wouldn't think she is nearly fifty,' the gallant husband said.

Dolly looking not a day over thirty-five withered him with an old-fashioned southern look. It was blistering.

Why do these Americans return each year? Why do they enjoy Wimbledon with the same frenzy of old boys returning to a school bun fight? Why do they savour their 'royal' stories with blatant relish?

'There is certainly an aura about Wimbledon that you find nowhere else and I think for that reason most of the players become very nostalgic. I work for an investment banking firm in Philadelphia but it seems round about the middle of June every year I start feeling nostalgic about Wimbledon. Just to be here and absorb the atmosphere again and see old friends. You just don't find it anywhere else.

'Whenever people ask me when I won I always say, "Coronation year, 1953. It was a big year for the Queen and for me." '

Seixas then lapses into his royal story.

'In 1953 I knew what to do but on my first appearance it was slightly different. I played John Bromwich, an old-time favourite from Australia, who was a very good player and one of Queen Mary's favourites.

'It was my very first time on the Centre Court. I knew that Bromwich had been through this before but like everyone else on their first time, I was a little in awe. Bromwich said:

' "It's quite simple, just go out and when we get half-way to the umpire's chair we turn round and lean over and bow like this. You go down when I do and come up when I back up."

'So out we went and I bowed way down from the waist and Bromwich of course just nodded his head. I kept waiting and looking round wondering when he was going to come up. Finally people started giggling. I could hear this ripple and I realised that I had overdone it a little. I think Queen Mary got a kick out of that because she came every day it seemed to me when I was playing for many years.

'There is another thing about coming back to Wimbledon—the veterans' doubles. It is not an official tournament in the sense that there is prize money or anything like that. It is really for fun in a way. It gives some of the older players something to do while they are here besides just watching. But I must say that when we got out on that court it is just as bloody as it used to be. We don't play as hard but we try just as much.'

Every year in the tent behind the secretary's lodge the veterans hold their own cocktail party with Borotra the doyen of them all.

'Hi, Budge . . . Where's Jack? . . . Well, what do you know, it's Fred . . . Did you bring Dolly? . . . Meet my sons . . .' the stories flow fast and furious, and time slips back—ten, twenty, thirty years.

Though Jack Kramer was the first man to wear shorts (1947) on the Centre Court, it was Ted Schroeder (1949 USA champion) who set the seal on the new look for men. He arrived from California with a spanking new wardrobe of extra slim cut shorts to be worn with a gym vest, socks and gym shoes.

During practice the shorts began to chafe his crotch until it was agony to play. Schroeder was desperate. All of them had been made by the same sports shop and were cut the same way, and he was due to play next day. By now the shops were shut.

Early the following morning Dennis Coombe, former New Zealand tennis player, and now a director of Slazengers, rang Simpsons of Piccadilly and arranged that a salesman and supply of shorts would be ready at 9am. Schroeder and Coombe arrived and the American got kitted up before going on to Queen's for practice.

Women players have broken bra straps, frilly panties have been in danger with weak elastic and zips have stuck at an awkward moment, but this was the first time a player would have had to scratch because of a scotched crotch. It was an experience every male player took to heart.

Gardnar Mulloy was always the self-styled 'bad boy' of the Americans. Nastase and Gimeno are choirboys by comparison.

'I stood up for my rights and I think they misunderstood me more than anything else. I'm the world's worst sport. Every time I lost it killed me.'

Today as a successful attorney and tennis director of the largest hotel in the world, the Fontainbleu, at Miami Beach, Gardnar Mulloy is more rational, less fiery and not so prone to blowing his top.

He is remembered in tennis circles as the man who threw his racket at a linesman at Queen's Club and as the only American non-champion to be made a life member of the All England Club. It is the kind of inexplicable reasoning that makes Wimbledon so appealing.

The incident at Queen's Club happened when Mulloy in a match against Rex Hartwig of Australia, twice questioned a linesman's decision whether a ball was in or out. In the end Mulloy threw his racket in the direction of the linesman, spat on the ground, picked up his racket and walked off.

To reporters Mulloy later said:

'I was robbed. I should have won. Your officiating stinks.'

When Pack Peart of the *Sunday Pictorial* wrote an article entitled 'The Miami Mouthpiece', Mulloy instructed his lawyers to begin an action for libel. He was advised against the suit and dropped it, but in anger cabled a piece to the *Miami Daily News* seeking to expose the myth of British sportsmanship.

'All one hears over here is what great sportsmen the British are. I've got news for you; the English are no better sports than the spectators in other countries, and, in my opinion, worse than some. And I've seen them all. The British talk about sportsmanship until they believe it. But they don't practise what they preach. It's like the guy who tells you how honest he is. Hold on to your watch! Sportsmanship, like honesty, is not discussed.'

But all that is long ago and now a seasoned Mulloy remembers Wimbledon as the ex-head boy talks of his Alma Mater—bemused, tolerant, indulgent and proud. Like his story about the Queen.

'Years ago when I was at one of Lady Crosfield's garden parties a group of us started talking to Princess Elizabeth. She was on my left and I said:

' "Your Highness, we have never had the pleasure of seeing you at Wimbledon. We've seen King Gustav, we've seen your father play here when he was Duke of York, your grandmother was a great patron but we have never had the pleasure of seeing you here. I wonder why?"

'Lady Crosfield was a bit upset and quickly interrupted:

' "My dear Mr Mulloy, you must understand that the royal family has many calls on its time and it is not always possible for them to do everything."

'Being a smart American, I replied: "Oh, I didn't understand. I thought maybe she couldn't get tickets and I would be happy to provide her with some of mine."

'The first time Princess Elizabeth came to Wimbledon as Queen was in 1957 and saw the finals when Budge Patty and I won the medals for the doubles. When she handed me mine, I bowed and said:

' "Your Highness, it's delightful to receive this cup from you and I was just wondering if you remembered meeting me."

'She said: "Yes, Mr Mulloy, I remember meeting you very well. As a matter of fact I had difficulty getting in today because you forgot to leave the tickets." '

When Gardnar Mulloy won the doubles with Budge Patty against Neale Fraser and Lew Hoad of Australia, he was only five months off forty-four years of age. A previous title winner, A. W. Gore, was forty-one when he won the men's singles for the third time in 1908. Their win was also the first time an unseeded pair or player had won a championship.

'I was sitting in the competitors' stand the other day when a messenger came up and said that the chairman of the All England wanted to see me at 6.30pm. I had a prior dinner engagement and I told him so. A little later Herman David came back and said that it was very important that I be there, so I broke the dinner engagement and went to the meeting. I had my tail between my legs. I thought they were going to bawl me out over something. I couldn't think what I had done. I hadn't sent in my ticket. I hadn't pushed someone through the gate. I hadn't raised hell. I just couldn't figure it out. So I got there in plenty of time, and Herman David was very serious and stern, and said:

' "There's a picture outside we want you to look at."

'So I went outside and looked at this picture, big picture of the Queen giving Budge Patty and me the trophies for winning the doubles in 1957. So I came back and said: "That's a picture of us."

'He said: "Yes, because that was such a delightful match and you've been around so long, we'd like to make you an honorary member of the All England Club."

'So I was a little excited about that. It's quite an honour and I was just speechless about the whole thing.'

They all come back. I found Budge Patty, who now lives in Switzerland, sitting on the carpeted staircase up to the office of the secretary Major Mills. A serene man with a lazy smile that slowly spreads across his face.

'I have been in four finals here and probably one of the things I find really good about Wimbledon is that because you are treated so much better than you are in any tournament, it makes it possible to easily get into top mental condition. Unless you are a very experienced player it is possible to get out on the Centre Court and lose the match and not even realise how because of the electricity that is out there. When you walk out there you can feel the atmosphere, the crowd is all tensed, they're nervous, they're waiting for the action to start. This relays to the player. It's a terrific feeling.

'I remember when I was playing there with Pauline Betz in the mixed doubles, and I went wide, wide, wide. I was playing in the back court and one of the opponents hit a smash, a very angled smash, and it was close to the nets. It bounced terribly high and it went over towards the tribune so I ran up, jumped over the barrier and went up one or two rows. I hit the ball and got it back but as the racket came down, clunk, right on the head of some poor old man.

'I looked at his head and saw that I had cut him right on the forehead. Blood was pouring down his face but I had to go on playing the match. I knew he would be taken care of by the stewards.

'When I came off the court there was the man with his head all bandaged up. He said: "Mr Patty, I would like to thank you for hitting me on the head."

'I said: "God Almighty, thank me. I am so sorry. It was terrible."

'He said: "No, no, not at all, because the All England Club has told me that as long as I decided not to sue or claim damages they would give me Centre Court seats for the rest of the tournament, otherwise I would never have had them. So thank you again for hitting me on the head." '

Of the other Americans of that era, Billy Talbert is a senior vice-president of the Security US Bank Note Corporation and is also chairman of the US open championships at Forest Hills in California for the third year running. Tony Trabert runs a summer tennis camp for children as well as manufacturing business interests. Elsworth Vines gave up his tennis career at its zenith and became a golf professional, reaching the top in two sports. Don Budge is a tennis professional in Acapulco in Mexico and Bobby Riggs was with a photographic company and is now retired living in California.

CHAPTER 19

Great 'Little Mo'

The day before she died of cancer in 1968 in Dallas, Maureen ('Little Mo') Connolly, one of the three immortal greats in women's tennis, wrote out a list of books that she wanted her daughters to read when she was no longer with them. It was a mixed bag of the classics, the best in contemporary literature, books on sport and on the theatre. The list was given to Cindy and Brenda to be cherished by them for the rest of their lives. 'Little Mo' was under heavy medication and knew that her hours were coming to an end.

It is typical of the completeness, maturity and dedication of this phenomenal woman who was then only thirty-four years of age.

'She was the most mature human being that I have ever met,' says Mary Hardwick Hare, the former British Wightman Cup player who now lives in Chicago.

Mary Hare was with Maureen Connolly on that day she made the list and remembers vividly her courage.

'The cancer had spread to all over her body but she was in complete charge of herself until the end. It was absolute hell for her as she had to have injections of pain-killer.'

They had first met in 1945.

'I was still playing pretty good tennis and I was in San Diego in California. They said to me:

' "There is this young girl, little Maureen Connolly only eleven years old, will you have a set with her?"

'I said, "Yes, of course, I would love to have a set with her."
'And they said, "She can only play between twelve o'clock and
two o'clock because she is at school."
'We had our set and when we were finished, she said:
' "Thank-you-very-much-I-enjoyed-it-and-one-day-I-am-going-
to-be-the-world's-greatest-tennis-player."
'Now, if you think that's precocious, it sounds like it but it
wasn't. Because she played just the same then, only not quite so
good, but the same type of strokes as when she won Wimbledon.
We became tremendous friends, and my husband Charles and I
are on the Maureen Connolly Foundation which has been created
in America for the development of young girl tennis players.'

No one suspected that, in fact, Maureen Connolly Brinker was
ill. It began when she went to hospital to have an examination as
she wanted a son to complete her family of two daughters. The
cancer was immediately detected and she had her first operation.
Five years later she was dead.

Maureen Connolly began her tennis life as a ball girl—a small,
determined, funny little girl with a burning determination to
succeed. She entered her first tournament when only ten years of
age at the La Jolla Club in San Diego. Soon she became a pupil
of the great 'Teach' Tennant, who guided Alice Marble to the
Wimbledon title. She liked the plucky girl she saw on the court
with her grim little face and indomitability to be the greatest.

Maureen was dubbed 'Little Mo' in contrast to the world's
most powerful battleship the USS *Missouri* which was known as
'Big Mo'. Off court she was a sunny, normal girl but on court
she had a ruthlessness that was frightening.

To her close English friends Heather and Clarence Jones she
once said:

'My ambition is to play perfect tennis, then I will *always* win.
I am so intent on playing perfectly when I am on court that usually
I am scarcely aware who my oppponent is.'

At sixteen years of age she won the US championship, a year
short of her tennis idol, Helen Wills. It was 1952 when she
arrived in England to capture Wimbledon. There was never a

doubt in her mind nor that of 'Teach' Tennant. They set up camp and began the gruelling days of last minute training for the Centre Court.

'Little Mo' arrived to a ready-made fan club. The crowds were hypnotised as she walked with her bobbity-bob head along the back line. She had the big match temperament like the new young Californian star Chris Evert. She played without a smile, without showing any emotion. When she was winning her head bobbed forwards and backwards like a chicken pecking corn. When she was having to fight, her movements became more laboured and slower.

In that final match in one hour and five minutes she wore down that seasoned green-eyed blonde from Oklahoma, Louise Brough. Her hard hitting drives whipped the court, that right forehand which had begun as a left hand, as a child, sent the balls screeching down the lines.

If spectators had wondered whether this compact tennis machine was human after all, they relished the way she patted her lucky bracelet and went in for the kill just when victory was in sight.

Although she was an ardent Catholic, Maureen Connolly relied on her heart-shaped bracelet locket and Chinese ring, which she always wore, rather than prayer. She could not play without them. On one occasion when the locket was lost she refused to play. Only when it had been found in a street gutter and bent back into shape so that she could wear it, would she play.

At the end of her match against Louise Brough she let out a little screech like any child and bobbity-bobbed off court, her toes turned in like a teddy bear. So compact, so intense, so alone. In her dressing-room she wept.

'Little Mo' returned to Wimbledon the following year. More assured and more powerful than ever. Her singles when she beat her close friend Doris Hart 8–6, 7–5 is still classed as one of the finest women's matches ever played.

By now she had broken with 'Teach' Tennant, the brilliant woman who had moulded her into the tennis classic that she had become. After catching cold in her practice clothes while training, a top orthopaedic consultant was called in and diagnosed fibrositis and a torn muscle. 'Teach' begged her not to withdraw as her whole career was in jeopardy. Maureen, aided by her mother, decided to go it alone. For both the teacher and her seventeen-year-old star pupil it was a devastating decision.

During her training 'Little Mo' devised her own plan. She was so utterly physically and mentally spent at the excitement of preparing herself that after her practice she used to go back to her hotel and drop into a deep sleep.

After winning the title she continued to play but told Mary Hardwick Hare:

'I'll never do it again. I'll never play after the title. You just cannot do it physically or emotionally. It takes too much out of you.'

When later in the year 'Little Mo' won the American singles title for the third successive year, she became the first woman to win the championships of France, Australia, England and the USA all in one year. Like 'Big Mo' she was invincible.

In 1954 she was teamed up once more with Louise Brough who was returning after a year's absence to reach her sixth Wimbledon final since 1946.

By now the Wimbledon crowds were not so generous. They rarely seemed on her side and began to wait to see how many points she would drop. They had become impatient of her assured success. 'Little Mo' had never listened to the crowd. Every inch the champion, she played superb tennis winning for the third year running 6–2, 7–5.

A few weeks later Maureen Connolly went riding back in San Diego when a cement mixer crashed into her horse. In that split second her only thought was whether she would ever play tennis again.

'If she had never had this accident she probably would never have married Norman Brinker. She was only twenty and would have turned professional. While she was in hospital he went to see her and the romance which had been broken off when he was riding with the American Olympic Equestrian team and she was busy winning Wimbledon, was on again,' Mary Hardwick Hare recalls.

Backed by all her tennis friends, Maureen sued the trucking company and was awarded 95,000 dollars damages. Jack Kramer, then running his Kramer Circus, was one of the chief witnesses. One of the first things that Maureen Connolly did when she received her compensation cheque was to visit 'Teach' Tennant and repay her. She handed a cheque over and they never spoke again.

'Teach' Tennant who twice in her life knew rejection from the stars she had made—Alice Marble and Maureen Connolly—still lives in California with her memories. She is now almost blind.

In a wedding dress made by Teddy Tinling, 'Little Mo' married Norman Brinker in 1955. The following year she returned to Wimbledon to report ' The Fortnight' for a national newspaper. She was as withering with words as she had been with play:

'Top class tennis, the most graceful of all games, degenerated into a brutal serve and volley affair. Gone are the long thrilling rallies with which Don Budge and Jack Kramer brought the crowd to their feet before they ended in a perfectly timed *coup de grace* volley. Now there is no preparation for the winning shot. Every ball is a winner or a miserable parody of one that throws away a point.'

And those two daughters, Cindy now fifteen and Brenda two years younger, live with their father who has remarried, and has made a brilliantly successful career in the restaurant business. Cindy is already a champion having piled up sixty trophies, and Brenda who looks like 'Little Mo' is a promising junior.

Says Cindy: 'I know I'll never be as good as Mom. I just hope I can represent her in the best way.'

Page 135
Two triers: (*right*) Christine Truman (GB); (*below*) Anne Haydon Jones (GB), who struggled for fourteen years to get to the top, winning the ladies' singles in 1969

Page 136
Acrobatics at Wimbledon:
(*above*) Alfred 'Freddie'
Huber (Austria), a
likeable clown;
(*left*) Jaroslav Drobny
(Czechoslovakia), 1954
men's singles champion
after four hours and ninety
minutes of hard work

CHAPTER 20

Fashion Scene

When the word glamour was fresh and shining in the thirties Wimbledon abounded in beauty. Women players so pretty and feminine that they were surrounded by admirers on and off court.

Eileen Bennett—now Mrs 'Mousy' Forslind—with her silky voice, beguiling charm and ageless glamour is a regular visitor to 'The Fortnight'. She was the girl who dared to wear shorts for the first time in public.

'I was then designing clothes at Ifor, a shop in Conduit Street. At the annual pre-Wimbledon party given by Lady Crosfield I wore pale blue shorts. I had a long white coat on and was absolutely terrified to take it off. They were terribly respectable and not as we know them today. Much more like a divided skirt. Imagine how amazed I was when my photo was on the front page of all the newspapers the next day. But I still did not dare wear them at Wimbledon.'

It was Helen Jacobs who first wore them there when she arrived in 1934 from America.

'Shorts have proved very lucky to me ever since I played in them in the American final last year,' she announced. And for the first time all the women members of the Wightman Cup turned up in trim masculine-looking just above the knee shorts.

Tom Webster of the *Daily Mail* wrote:

'When the little darlings came striding on to the courts in their shorts they made our trousers feel longer than ever. Miss

Helen Jacobs looked taller in shorts than any man we could think of.'

Even the royal family joined the shorts-for-women controversy. At the British Industries Fair the Prince of Wales (the late Duke of Windsor) said:

'I see no reason on earth why any woman should not wear shorts for lawn tennis. They are very comfortable and quite the most practical costume for the game and I don't think the wearers lose anything in looks.'

A few days previously the Duchess of York (Queen Elizabeth the Queen Mother) had also given her approval. At a charity mannequin parade of tennis costumes down the age, she had seen Eileen Bennett wearing shorts and remarked:

'They are far more sensible.'

But a member of the Lawn Tennis Association at the Roehampton Club had other views against what he said was 'a disgusting sight'.

But shorts were here to stay. By 1956 they had begun to creep shorter. A notice was promptly placed in the women's dressing-room:

'If shorts get any shorter they won't be allowed any longer.'

Three champions through the years who steadfastly refused to switch over to wearing fashion conscious dresses were Alice Marble ('Girl of the Golden Gate'), Angela Mortimer and Althea Gibson.

It is a long step from the shorts of the thirties to the fashion scene of today, and the person most responsible for the change is Teddy Tinling.

He walked along the flower-fringed promenade in front of the main offices of the club—6ft 6in tall, distinguished, cadaverous. The head was shaved, now strangely domed. The eyes were deep set, keen, piercing.

He acknowledged greetings regally. The new Wimbledon young in their droopy, flowered skirts and Dr Scholl shoes scarcely noticed him but the veterans turned and stared and nudged each other.

'That's Teddy Tinling,' they said reverently.

Although he has no official status today, Teddy Tinling is part of the very structure of Wimbledon and one of the great characters who embellish this successful anachronism.

There were the days back in the thirties when he strode the Centre Court like Colossus always immaculate in his pin-stripe suit. Today he wears a trendy grey silk suit bound with aubergine lizard skin with bow tie to match. The jacket is reminiscent of an Edwardian dandy and the trousers pipe cleaner skinny. He wears it with superb aplomb. It is his defiant answer to middle age.

So many of the charming nuances of Wimbledon have emanated from Tinling's facile brain during the forty-five years he has been associated with it. It is he alone who brought the complete transformation in the way women tennis players dressed. He made them look feminine, pretty, tennis ballerinas.

Shocked that the players did not have a hot meal during the entire fortnight he campaigned for them until this was changed. Today they can choose from several hot dishes including steak and lamb cutlets.

Every year when the women finalists walk to the Centre Court on their great day it is due to Teddy Tinling's connivance that they carry the bouquets which are traditionally sent to their dressing-room by the All England Club. It transforms tennis Amazons into vulnerable women and the crowds love it.

We were sitting pre-Wimbledon in Teddy Tinling's studio-factory near the Hammersmith fly-over while he was pinning up a rush order for clothes to be worn by the women players in the Virginia Slims circuit in America. It was a relatively new commission. He was thinner, keener than when we had last met many years ago and obviously enjoying the challenge of working for a highly competitive American company. His zest was infectious.

'I love the Americans. They are so keen and receptive to new ideas,' he said. In that clipped, articulate voice of his—more often with a mouthful of pins—he told me of his early days. Time slipped back to the twenties and thirties when tennis was still a leisured and graceful art, and people were rich and elegant.

'It seems to me that fate sets a scene into which one can only fit one way. I had asthma and was in bed most of my life until I was twelve. That was my scene. What does one do if you have an active mind? I always wanted to make something out of nothing. I had a governess who had spent a great deal of her life in India and was therefore a wonderful needlewoman. Her one thing when looking after her charge was to teach it needlework even if it was a boy. It might just as well have been someone else whose natural ability was carpentry who would have had me hammering away. But the fact is that I was taught to sew when I was about three.

'My governess was very constructive minded. I wanted to sew, so why not make something for my teddy bear. When I put the first garment I made on the bear it couldn't move its arms. I said, "This is nonsense. What is the matter with the sleeve?"

'So from this stems my dedication to clothes that move. All my clothes must work. My mother observed me absorbed by movement in design and encouraged me. I was either going to be a musician, which she hoped for, or to be a dress designer which I wanted to be.

'So my youth went by with sewing indoors and playing tennis outdoors, to make me stronger. I was suddenly launched into life by my father having a financial crash. Tennis was the first thing on my doorstep to earn money. The other fatalistic thing was my association with Suzanne Lenglen. Her philosophy is the thing that I project every day of my life.'

During the next few years Tinling was to umpire the French star in 104 matches as well as to become a devoted friend.

Because of his height and his flamboyant temperament, Teddy Tinling quickly became known in the Riviera tennis world as a character. It was while he was umpiring in France in 1927 that Dudley (Major) Larcombe, then secretary of the All England Club, sent for him and asked him if he would like to take up some sort of a job during the Wimbledon championships. On that basis he arrived at the All England Club and was part of the temporary staff with which Major Larcombe surrounded himself.

'There were twelve of us who did it all for nominal money as we loved it dearly and only met during that fortnight. Larcombe taught everyone that nothing but the best could be acceptable. The moment he observed that it was not the best it was good-bye.'

Tinling, among other jobs, was immediately made liaison officer between the committee and the players. He was there to see that if there was anything that the players were critical of or wanted improved he should immediately report to the secretary. This included being a 'call boy' to the Centre Court, so that no players would be late. He physically escorted them out into the arena.

The new players always underestimated the time it took to get round the grounds of Wimbledon as their restaurant is at one end and their dressing-rooms at the other. Two or three days before the championship opened they were given a Tinling 'special'—a kind of pep talk about clothes, manners and such mundane things as where to find the nearest lavatory.

It was not until 1947 that Teddy Tinling made his first dress for Wimbledon. He had dressed his mother since he was a teenager and made Wimbledon champion Dorothy Round's wedding dress but the tennis dress as we know it today was unknown. The nearest anyone had seen to fluid, action lines were the tennis dresses Patou made for Suzanne Lenglen.

'It was in 1947 when Joy Gannon, now Joy Mottram, was making her début. We had had Eileen Bennett, followed by Kay Stammers, followed by Joy Gannon. Totally English—milk and roses complexions—couldn't be anything else in the world but English.

'Mrs Gannon came to Gordon Lowes where I was working while on demob leave and asked me if I could make something different and specially for Joy. I remembered Suzanne's revolution in tennis wear by scorning corsets and adding coloured accessories to traditional white frocks. Indeed her progressive reign made bright jerseys and rainbow-hued bandeaux as much a part of conventional tennis attire as white dresses themselves.

'I designed Joy Gannon's dresses with a tiny band of pink

round the bottom of one and with a similar band of blue on the other. She was very pleased. No one even noticed them at the time but they were the forerunners of the dresses we see today.'

The following year (1948) Britain's Betty Hilton, a very dominant personality, asked Tinling to make her a dress with even more colour. This he did and she wore it in the Wightman Cup. Betty had a shattering defeat and only won two games in her match. Mrs Wightman subscribed to the view held by everyone that her unconventional dress had put her off her game! She then asked Kay Stammers to see that the English girls did not wear any colour the following day. This threw several of the women players but as Teddy Tinling explains:

'Mrs Wightman had known me all my life and we were on kissing terms. I christened her Queen Canute on that day. "If you think you can hold back the tide, good luck. But you won't. Colour has come to stay." '

Twenty-six years later when Teddy Tinling was sitting with Mrs Wightman on her eightieth birthday in Cleveland, Ohio, she was sporting enough to remind him of the incident and acknowledge that he was right.

By 1949 colour and Tinling had come to stay in the fashion world. The dresses he had made for Joy Gannon and Betty Hilton had already caused a stir in the United States and had been featured in the fashion columns of *American Lawn Tennis* which was written then by a young player, Gertrude Augusta Moran—'Gussy' for short.

What more natural than that she wrote to Teddy Tinling and said, as she was coming to Wimbledon would he make her dresses for her. The briefing was straightforward, if a trifle unconventional.

'I love colour and always wear it even in my hair ribbon—and I even have Red Indian blood.'

Miss Moran arrived in England—a coltish-legged, nut brown girl with that special glowing all-American look. She had no more or no less personality than the other players but Tinling-plus-Wimbledon was to make her name a household word over the next six months. In short, the man made her lace-edged panties to go under her white tennis dress and Wimbledon gave them the traditional setting to make world news.

Nowadays with frilly panties on every court the eye expects such frivolity but in the stern 1940s there was even a notice in the dressing-rooms barring colour. That the coarse, white lace was sewn on as an afterthought makes the story no less piquant.

'Gussy'—she had yet to earn her prefix 'Gorgeous'—wore her panties at the Hurlingham Sunday party before Wimbledon. She was knocking up on one of the lesser courts with Gardnar Mulloy when a photographer caught a flash of the lace. Brown bare legs and lace panties—he could not go wrong. The picture was sent back to Fleet Street in a matter of minutes.

Monday morning 'Gussy' was front page news. 'Gussy' hitting away like mad showing her most dashing tennis strokes, but it was the streaks of lace-edged leg that made the headlines. 'Gorgeous Gussy' all the picture editors simultaneously gave her the title and to this day Miss Moran now a successful radio commentator, with three broken marriages behind her, still bears the name.

'Gussy' did not wear the panties the first day at Wimbledon but Fleet Street kept the story going. Would she? Wouldn't she? Gertrude Augusta Moran (under tuition from Teddy Tinling, I suspect) played it cool. By the Wednesday the panties incident had grown into international proportions. Colonel Macaulay, the club secretary, advised his committee that he would inspect them to see what all the fuss was about.

Solemnly he and his assistant, Major David Mills, the present secretary, went to the ladies' dressing-room on the Tuesday night when everyone had gone home, to look for themselves. The panties were hanging with her dress. Recalling the affair from twenty-three years' distance, Duncan Macaulay told me:

'There was nothing very special about them at all. It was quite ordinary lace and seemed to be only tacked on. I didn't mind what she wore. The only thing I did mind was if she didn't wear any pants. In fact they were great fun and even Princess Marina liked them when she first saw them.'

When 'Gussy' began playing on the court, the crowd were

obviously mesmerised by the glimpses of lace. That day tennis fashion history had been made.

'I always credit Laurie Pignon of the *Daily Mail* who was then on the *Daily Sketch* for "Gussy's" lace,' Tinling told me. 'It was Laurie who said, "Oh, you must do something tremendously sexy for 'Gussy' Moran."

'He planted the seed in my mind. The public were hungry for something away from regimentation. Everyone had seen nothing but uniformity and all that utility lark that had gone on for years in England. The American players who came to England after the war were practically indistinguishable. They wore the same shorts and shirts and hair styles. And they played the same sort of game.

' "Gussy" had asked me to make her something to wear under the new rayon jersey dress I had designed for her. The pants we made looked bare, unattractive. In irritation I told my fitter:

' "For goodness' sake put something attractive round the legs. We mustn't use colour, but surely we can find something which will show and yet be flatteringly feminine."

'That is how the lace panties were born. The niggling attention to detail was not impelled by any erotic urge, but simply by my determination to have a job properly finished to my personal standards.

' "Gussy" beat Betty Wilford comfortably in straight sets and went back to her hotel suite to face the obligations of her new status. In the next five days she was called upon to visit hospitals, open fêtes, give her name to a race-horse and an aircraft, judge beauty contests and become the central attraction of countless unlikely occasions.'

'Gussy's' lace panties still ranks as one of the greatest public relation jobs of all time. The fact that she never reached the form predicted for her did not matter. 'Gussy' and glamour were synonymous.

This was the beginning of the final break away of Teddy Tinling's professional association with the All England Lawn Tennis and Croquet Club. A few days later in a public speech at a tennis party, the late Sir Louis Greig, who was then chairman, had thundered:

'I will never allow Wimbledon to become a stage for a designers' stunts.'

Tinling, who was present, was desperately hurt. He had no redress then and after considering it overnight handed in his resignation.

Through the years that followed Teddy Tinling was to continue to design fashion that made headlines at Wimbledon. There were the golden panties for the American 'Greek Goddess', Karol Fageros. Genuine eighteen carat cloth-of-gold undershorts, overlaid with lace, that had to be kept locked away in secrecy in the private office of Mrs Nellie Twynam who was in charge of the number one dressing-room. The panties, in fact, were worn only once at Wimbledon simply because they scratched, but it kept the fashion writers sizzling for days.

There were the pale mauve linings worn by Maria Bueno, the graceful Brazilian champion. Mauve used on a tennis court years in advance of the great mauve fashion wave that is still hitting the High Street all over the world.

The next year it was an orangeade championship for Maria. The next, the fateful semi-final when Maria's bright pink panties were said by some to have dazzled her opponent Vera Sukova of Czechoslovakia.

Looking round the courts, delighting in Chris Evert's duckling bottom of yellow frills, how innocent it all is. How desperately pedantic on the part of a few stuffy committee members to try to forbid a bit of frivolous fun. Tennis is now show business.

And so the fashion saga goes on. Last year we had Rosie Casals and her forbidden 'advertising dress'. To the public it was just another 'fun dress', a short shift with some rather garish embroidery. But to Captain Mike Gibson, the referee, it spelt that forbidden word advertising. The embroidery was in fact stylised initials of the Virginia Slims circuit in America.

Rosie was unrepentant when reprimanded and Tinling explanatory:

'I designed the dress for Miss Casals to wear on TV in America. I told her that I didn't think it would be suitable for Wimbledon —it was too startling for an English audience. For Wimbledon I designed several white dresses for her, but a star's choice of dress when she goes on court is a personal matter. It is entirely her own business.'

The girls from America, led by 'women's lib' Billie Jean King, are campaigning for more and more colour and less restrictions in their clothes in world tournaments.

If anyone can bring about a solution to Wimbledon's only colour problem—the fashion one—then it is Teddy Tinling. He has the flair, the taste, and the lifelong experience of the Wimbledon way of thinking.

CHAPTER 21

A Quartet of
Champions

Two of the most exotic personalities in the sixties on the
Centre Court were the brilliant Maria Bueno from Brazil
and Althea Gibson, the first negro to win Wimbledon.
Maria with her tanned skin and fluid limbs brought a breath-
taking kind of grace that had not been seen since the Spanish
Lili de Alvarez. She looked like an exotic Siamese cat as she
roamed the court. She caught the public's imagination in the same
vivid way as Olga Korbut, the seventeen-year-old little Russian,
did in the gymnastic hall at the last Olympic Games. Maria was
sinuous, sensuous and feminine.

When Maria arrived at Wimbledon in 1958 she was only eighteen. She had won the Italian championships beating Britain's Shirley Bloomer before going on to the French championships. Rumours
of her super-star quality had already arrived at Wimbledon.

Born the daughter of a veterinary surgeon in Sao Paulo her
father insisted that along with her tennis career she must have a
proper vocation. With this in mind and implicitly obeying her
parents, the year before her European début had been a ruthless
one. Her day began at 2am when she studied until breakfast time
and tennis practice. Then off to school until 4pm and home again
to study until just before midnight.

Maria had never been formally coached. She was a natural

147

tennis genius who began playing as a girl of ten years of age. Her brother Pedro, who often practised against her, also became an international star. This adored brother and sister relationship has existed right through Maria's life. She wore his ring to remind her that he was thinking of her. To be separated from Pedro and her parents for any length of time was physically hurtful to Maria. Tennis families tend to be clannish and there have been many famous brother and sister relationships but perhaps none so emotionally strong as Maria and Pedro Bueno.

In the 1959 championship Maria found herself up against Darlene Hard of the USA whose capers had always delighted the fans. Playing an inspired game this wisp of a girl commanded uncanny strength as she delivered her brilliant penetrating service to win 6–4, 6–3. The Centre Court went mad.

Maria herself was dazed but even more excited when she realised that it was Saturday afternoon and she had no dress suitable for the Wimbledon Ball that night when she would take the floor with Alex Olmedo, the men's champion from the USA.

'Of course you must have a dress,' Duncan Macaulay told her. 'Leave it to me. We will fix it.'

After her press interview Maria was whisked off with a girl member of the All England staff to a boutique in Wimbledon which the owner specially opened and there she chose a tawny-brown georgette dress. The All England temporarily footed the bill until Colonel Macaulay presented it to the Brazilian officials.

'She's a wonderful champion and a credit to your country. Now you must pay the bill,' he argued.

And they did.

Maria returned to win Wimbledon the following year, defending her title against Sandra Reynolds of South Africa.

Such is the magic of winning a Wimbledon championship that for the second time Maria returned to a royal welcome. She was given a ticker tape drive, the jockey club gave her a car, a 60ft statue of her was erected at the Tiete tennis club and there was a special issue of a commemorative stamp.

Had ill health and an unstable temperament not dogged the

following years Maria Bueno may have done a hat trick at Wimbledon. The strain of top rank playing and her own unpredictable ill health showed itself the following year when she was ill for four months with hepatitis, an inflammation of the liver.

Drugged by the glamour of international tennis, Maria returned to win Wimbledon again in 1964 from Margaret Smith of Australia. The following year a surgical operation on her left knee put her out of competitive tennis. She returned to Wimbledon in 1968 but now an elbow dogged her with bad luck. She was beaten in the quarter-finals by Nancy Richey of the USA.

Maria Bueno, considered by many to be the most graceful of all women tennis players, has not returned to Wimbledon since. She still lives in Sao Paulo where she helps coach young tennis players and lives on her memories of when they called her 'The Queen of Wimbledon'.

Few people in 1957 who saw Althea Gibson, the first American negro to win Wimbledon, realised her immense struggle to the top. When she was presented to the Queen who was in the royal box that day as well as the Duke and Duchess of Kent, this tall, rangy girl, with the beautiful limbs and attractive colouring, was so overcome that she stepped back sideways so that she would not turn her back on the Queen.

It was the culmination of a career that began in a small town in South Carolina, was nurtured in the jungle atmosphere of Harlem and finally brought her to Wimbledon in 1956.

Like most negroes, Althea is the complete athlete and could have reached the top in soft-ball and basket-ball. That she played like a man is understandable as she had the complete muscular co-ordination of the great Kenyan athletes of last year's Olympics as well as a dedicated tough mental approach.

The way up had not been easy nor without humiliation.

As Mary Hardwick Hare remembers:

'Being English and living in the States I got into the situation of giving practice to many of the up and coming players. This is how I came to play with Althea when she was allowed to play in her first American coloured tournament. She was not allowed to play in any ordinary tournament as this was the beginning of the situation with the coloured people.

'The authorities picked out to play in Chicago because it was neutral. It wasn't New York. It wasn't California. It wasn't the south. But the strange thing is that Althea was not allowed to change in the club-house and I had to find somewhere else so that she could.

'She also had to have some practice before the tournament and again because I wasn't American they chose me. Nothing was easy for Althea in those days.'

Her championship final in 1957 remains one of the great finals at Wimbledon. She had much less charisma than some of the finalists, but the Centre Court has always been fanatically on the side of the underdog. They willed Althea to win in her match against Darlene Hard.

At the Wimbledon Ball that night Althea made history. She is the only champion to have taken the microphone and sung. During her college days while studying for her BSc, she used to sing with the local band.

Althea Gibson was to retain her title in 1958 playing against Britain's Angela Buxton.

Back in the States after her triumphant Wimbledon the pressures put on Althea Gibson were enormous. With great dignity and following her own guideline 'Never Shirk Responsibility', she gave all she had towards furthering a better relationship between negro and white America.

She linked up with the 'golden goddess' Karol Fageros in an exhibition tour for the Harlem Globetrotters. Her tennis was still superb but the climate of America was not ready for such a mixed tour. It was not the qualified success it should have been.

When Althea's interest in tennis began to wane, she switched to golf with the same ruthless determination she had shown in tennis. She now plays in a prominent women's golf circuit.

The 1960s also produced a bumper crop of efficient British women players—Angela Mortimer, Ann Haydon and Christine Truman. They behaved impeccably on and off court. They looked

human. They were not invulnerable. They could have been anyone's sister.

As Mrs Biddy Godfree, who has seen the whole spectrum of
women players over the last fifty years says:

'Looking back over the years I think the young girls have
almost always behaved beautifully on court. Particularly our
English girls. Funnily enough, I can't say the same about the
men.'

The year Angela Mortimer (Barrett) won Wimbledon—1961—
she came away with £20 in prize money. Last year Billie Jean
King, USA, winner of the women's singles received £1,800. But
Angela's memories are not bitter.

'Playing tennis enriched my life so enormously. I would never
have had all those wonderful trips and tours in places like South
America and Australia otherwise.'

Talking to the late Godfrey Winn she explained her tennis
philosophy and why she did not marry until she was twenty-nine:

'I married later than many girls. I only had eyes for the game.
We had very little money and it often meant getting up early to
practise at a time when the courts were free. But I didn't mind
that, and I sometimes can't help feeling now that the new lot have
it too easy. I sometimes wonder, too, what would have happened
if I never won. It would have broken my heart.'

Angela who was married at St Mary's, the church beyond the
All England grounds to John Barrett, a captain of the English
Davis Cup team, now has two children and has given up serious
tennis.

'We both try too hard when we are playing together. It's
rather a strain. I don't think, myself, husbands and wives should
play together. At least not in tournaments.'

Like so many of the tennis 'greats' Ann Haydon Jones was
plagued with ill health. As a child of eleven she contracted nephritis
the dreaded kidney disease. Six months in bed destroyed her sense
of balance and control of her legs. Her parents, both internation-
ally famous in table tennis, were determined to bring her back to
normal childhood. They encouraged her with a new game—a plank

balanced over a petrol drum. For hours she would practise balancing over the drum. When she fell off her parents were there to laugh and help her on again.

They began a programme of stamina building that was to take Ann Haydon Jones to victory on the Centre Court in her 1969 final against Billie Jean King.

Before the most partisan crowd since Christine Truman met Angela Mortimer in the 1961 final, Ann Jones faced the American. Billie Jean with her built-in distrust of Wimbledon had not only to fight for every point but found herself up against a hostile Centre Court. The crowd rustled and fidgeted. They chatted like nervous budgerigars. Billie Jean became ruffled as she faced the most underrated woman player in the world. She dropped a curtsy in disgust to unruly spectators. She lost that brilliant concentration, so much an integral part of her game.

In contrast the British girl, charged with a new dynamic confidence, changed her normal defensive role for one of attack. The score ended 3–6, 6–3, 6–2 and the crowd roared its approval for Ann. There probably never has been, nor ever will be, a more unassuming champion.

'I never set my heart on winning Wimbledon. There are other things in life. No doubt when I won it it was important simply because it is the ultimate in tennis and it made me more complete. But if I hadn't won it, it would have made no difference to me. Now I like looking after the baby and gardening.'

Coming from Ann Haydon Jones the remark was sincere.

CHAPTER 22

Christine, the Darling of Wimbledon

I n tennis more than any other sport it is the character and the temperament of the player that counts almost as much as his or her tennis skill. To the Wimbledon fans, Christine Truman represented everything that was decent, wholesome, English. When she first burst on the tennis scene she was a gangling teenager with the kind of face one finds in a school nativity play as the Virgin Mary. Totally serene, totally secure with a quiet inner happiness.

The Truman family with its six children is a uniquely self-contained one. Each child was encouraged to follow some kind of sport. Christine was just eleven when she announced to the family that she wanted to win Wimbledon, and at thirteen she won the *Evening News* competition at Wimbledon and caught the eye of Dan Maskell.

'It was her astonishing concentration and determination to chase the ball,' he recalls. 'It was quite unreal, un-English.'

Complete with mother she arrived on the Wimbledon scene just sixteen years of age and immediately became a favourite. Sports columnists coyly referred to her as 'The Darling of Wimbledon'. This was partly because of her youth, fresh schoolgirl looks, natural introspection and modest court behaviour. She fitted the pattern of sterling British sportsmanship.

Christine had her own fanatically loyal following. She is the only player at Wimbledon whom people left their Centre Court seats to watch when she was playing on an outer court. And that final match against Angela Mortimer in 1961 remains one of the most moving finals of all time.

Speaking of it today Christine holds no rancour, no bitterness.

'Oh, yes, I regret that I didn't win simply because if you work hard at anything you want it to be a success. It is a question of personal pride. I was almost there. I was leading 6–4, 4–3, 40–30 when I fell. I just slipped because I had been having trouble with my ankle.'

Throughout that vast Centre Court arena there was hushed horror as she lay there fighting with herself to get up.

'If only it had been possible for someone to say to me "Keep going" I would have been all right. It was not so much my ankle that hurt but the shock I got. From then on my concentration had gone. I only won one point in the next five games.'

How many players have had the same traumatic experience? When a call from the sideline turned a game of defeat into victory? Who can blame Mrs Gloria Connors, the American extrovert tennis mother who shouted last year to her brilliantly erratic nineteen-year-old son Jim:

'Yippee. Let's go, Jimbo baby.'

And while the crowd was recoiling she lashed out again:

'You're looking good, sweetheart.'

Even the invincible Maureen Connolly nearly faded out at her first Wimbledon. In her fourth round meeting on court 1 against Susan Partridge, when the odds were against her and she herself sensed a humiliating defeat, one clear call rang out. It was the strong, fresh young voice of a young American USAF boy on leave.

'Give 'em hell, Mo.'

Later Maureen was to say this flooded her with new hope and she came back fighting mad. She never met the voice but it remained as one of the most poignant moments in that great tennis career.

Christine Truman never did win Wimbledon. Like David Bedford, the athlete at last year's Olympics, she lacked the confidence to overcome her one weakness—a backhand drive—in important matches.

Dan Maskell says:

'The tragic thing is that I have a piece of film that shows she was capable of hitting a formidable backhand drive and had the acumen to win but when it came to match play she lacked the confidence. I tried every psychological trick I knew and even discussed it with Dr Gregory, the medical practitioner attached to the All England Club, but we never broke through her natural reticence.'

Today as a mother of two children, Christine Truman Jarvis has no regrets. Never a social tennis player she now spends her time coaching schoolchildren in her home county of Essex. Of her life at Wimbledon she says:

'I would do it all again. I appreciate it more now having done something with my life but I suppose the thing is to keep everything in proportion. I am very happy now.'

CHAPTER 23

Twenty Years to Make a Court

When the gates are closed at Wimbledon on that final night and the last staff stragglers have left, there is one figure still mooching round.

He's changed back from a smart lounge suit which he wears in the day with his air force tie, into his comfy Shetland polo-necked sweater. He is a small man with a mat of wavy steel-grey hair, a silver-grey moustache that looks as though it is stuck on the leathery brown face with glue. Each hair so immaculate. The face has lines and crags that seem to have been etched with a stone-mason's tooler, and the deep set eyes reveal nothing. He is a 'loner'.

This, then, is the head groundsman, Robert Twynam, who grows the 10,800 square yards of grass at Wimbledon, who has walked this emerald plot for fifty years and knows more about growing tennis grass than any man in the world.

As one member of the committee explained:

'He can be awkward, he speaks his mind, but Bob Twynam is fine. He treats each blade of grass as an individual with its own needs, its own destiny and its own right to grow on this blessed piece of lawn.'

Mr Twynam began life as a ball boy in the 1925 championships after a brief and not too happy period as a messenger for the GPO pedalling his bicycle round Chelsea and Battersea. In those days Wimbledon kept its own supply of resident ball boys, many of whom later became professional tennis teachers all over the world.

He ball-boyed for many of the 'greats' in those early days—Borotra, Cochet, Helen Wills Moody, Alice Marble. Today he still plays a reasonable game himself and has an interesting if unconventional knowledge of the game and its players.

He classes them all as toe-diggers, sliders, gentlemen and bloody menaces.

'Now Borotra, he was a terrible slider, something shocking . . . Falkenburg was one of the worst for that . . . it's the foreign players that are the worst offenders . . . the Australians play like gentlemen—clean feet.'

The foundation of the present courts was the work of Commander G. W. Hillyard, the then secretary of the All England Club. He had scoured the country examining the best croquet greens and decided on virgin seaside turf from Cumberland.

'It was actually full of live shrimps,' says his successor Colonel Macaulay, and it is the kind of improbable legend that Wimbledon thrives on.

Live shrimps or not, that first fortnight in the new grounds at Church Road was nearly a disaster. The rain pelted down mercilessly. The new turf was deliciously green but so lush and soft that the players skidded. A new grass had to be concocted.

Here Carters, the seed people, were called in to create what is now known as the Wimbledon mixture and today sells to the public at 50p a pound. With this new blend, the grass grew stronger and could be cut closer. During the season when the courts really take a beating, they may turn brown through loss of sap and lose their gloss but they remain hard and true and very fast.

'Other courts may be greener than ours,' says Twynam. 'I'm not interested in looks but how they behave. These lawns are made to be played on and not looked at. There is no nitrogen, sulphate of ammonia or phosphates used as forcing. I never overfeed them because they would get pappy and have no bloody guts in them. No mollycoddling. It must grow hard. That's what I'm after.'

Vic Seixas, the American veteran, who still comes over every year to play describes them as 'cement with fuzz on it'.

Even if you have the exact grass seed, any aspirant hoping to make an 'instant' Wimbledon is in for a shock.

'It takes twenty to thirty years to get a lawn like the Centre Court. Years of looking at it every day and seeing how you can improve it.'

Bob Twynam has kept a daily diary on the Centre Court for years and when the volumes were not returned to him by an American writer last year, he was desolate.

'May 1: light drizzle. Centre Court fine.

'May 2: nice bright sunshine. Centre Court OK.'

That's all. To Bob Twynam they were his life's heritage. His life's interest.

The structure of the Centre Court first begins 2ft down where for drainage, tops of tile drains are set in a herringbone pattern in the local clay. On top of this is 10in of clinker with 1in or so of fine ash on top. The next layer up is 1ft of loamy topsoil where the roots of the grass are nourished. A top dressing of fine soil forms the nursery bed for the tiny seeds.

The seeds are a mixture including Chewings Fescue and Oregan Browntop. There is also a good sprinkling of *Poa pratensis* which gives the light shimmer. Intermingled with this are several volunteers (the name for unwanted strains) that have blown over with the wind. But they don't stay long. Twynam and his men see to that.

Apart from their own hard-headed experience and the commonsense of the head groundsman and his staff, the All England can always call in experts from the National Turf Research Institute at Bingley near Bradford. This was an arrangement made many years ago.

One of the hazards at Wimbledon, which does not happen at many other international tennis clubs, is that the courts cannot be altered one inch. All the courts are static with the same base and sidelines. There is no question of moving them even half an inch should they show any wear.

'So it's make do and mend every year, and we begin work as soon as the championships are over. There are just 349 days left to get the Centre Court back into perfect condition. In the Centre Court it is a question of re-sowing after pruning the roots with a hand fork to let in air. The top is dusted with a little top dressing mixed with a Surrey loam and then rolled. A nice drop of gentle rain is all we need then for germination to begin. Late autumn we solid tine the turf with potato forks and top dress with loam again. Luting it's called. Just before the real winter we mow once or twice and then hope for a good cold winter to lift and aerate the roots.'

Because of its tiered seats, the Centre Court is the most difficult to keep in trim. It is a natural frost pocket with constricted air and sunshine in the dank winter months. It is for this reason, too, that a further top layer of seats, to accommodate more spectators, is not practical. The grass would just wither and eventually die.

Nothing as tortuous as mechanical lawn mowers have ever been allowed on the Centre Court and court number 1. The cutting and mowing is entirely done by hand. At Worple Road and in the pioneering days at Wimbledon a horse with felt slippers was used to pull the roller which weighs 2,500 pounds. As the new club arena in 1922 was built up around the Old Horse Roller (as it is called), it can never be removed without extensive damage to the walls. It is there as long as the All England Club stands. Nowadays a team of men pull it every day during the summer months. It takes Twynam's assistant, John Yardley, between the shafts and four men puffing behind.

'I like to roll every morning during the championships. The grass and court are firm enough but the roller gets a soft sheen on the court. That's what I like to see.'

The lawn mowers used are the same kind as seen every Saturday in millions of suburban gardens throughout Britain. They cost just under £50 and cut to three-sixteenths of an inch. During the growing period of mid-spring the cuts are made from side to side, but once the season is under way they are taken lengthwise. This explains the pleasing alternating stripes of shiny and mat grass which is especially noticeable if you sit in either the north or south stands.

During 'The Fortnight', Twynam is never far from the Centre Court. It does not happen often but when a player tears up a divot and it cannot be put back by stamping then Twynam is ready with his mending kit. A deep hole is filled with a mixture of clay and grass cuttings freshly prepared each morning. With surgical precision he knits it together working away with matchsticks. They are the hands of an artist craftsman and one feels each blade being caressed into place. Each piece of grass is an individual work of art.

There is something of the aesthetic in this man, too. He speaks reverently of 'hearing the grass grow', of 'making the ball speak', of 'getting down on my knees and praying to God the rain will stop'.

For the rest of the courts that do not need the petting that is given the Centre Court and court number 1, there is a nursery in the grounds where the turf for patching is grown. It takes three years before it can be used on the courts. Should a considerable patching job be needed, a turf is taken from the side of the court to replace where it is worn. At the nursery a pattern of grass is cut just as in dressmaking, and slid into place on the sideline. So skilfully is the job done that an amateur can hardly detect it.

During 'The Fortnight' the ground staff is increased by thirty-five students who work with regular club staff. Apart from cleaning up the litter, during play they man the tarpaulins that are needed to cover the courts. The Centre Court and court number 1 are sacrosanct and only handled by regular Wimbledon ground staff using the special mechanical derricks installed there. The covers are extremely heavy, with the one in the Centre Court weighing four tons when dry and considerably more when wet. But such is the split-second training of the staff, the covers are in place in a matter of minutes. It also means that the courts can be prepared during the morning even on a wet day.

Once a year it has to happen. Someone getting lost under the tarpaulins. When the courts become a bit damp, as they are bound to be between showers, they get slippery. If the students are in a hurry running with plimsolls, it is very easy to slip over. Because the tarpaulin is moving very fast, once you slip then you are underneath. The others keep on running. The trouble is that you lose your sense of direction because you are in the dark and you can't tell which way to go out. It's really very confusing. The tarpaulin is so heavy you can't stand up but just have to creep out on your hands and knees.

'We had it on the number 1 court one year and the crowd watching were in absolute hysterics because what you can see is a small bump moving about under the canvas and everybody else is convulsed until he gets out. There is not really anything you can do, I mean, but he'll come out in the end. In the middle you can't hear anything but nearer the edges you can. The other chaps don't try and direct you, quite the opposite, in fact. They try to stop you escaping. They think it is a hell of a joke as it is one of those traditional Wimbledon things. One year it happened right in front of the television cameras on number 1—they tracked the bump all the way until it emerged,' explained Dr Grover.

After early morning tea at 6.30, each man goes to his job. The whole operation like everything else is highly organised into subgroups who are on what is called 'baskets'. Their job is to go round and pick up all the big piles of rubbish that the other students have swept together, and put them into huge dustbins which are carried to the big tip.

At eleven, armed with brooms they spread themselves right across the main concourse at the South West Gate and then in unison swish their way through the South East Gate. It is a pretty impressive sight.

The Centre Court is only used twice a year apart from the championship fortnight. There is the match played by four lady members of the club usually forty-eight hours before the championship begins.

'Just to see how she is shaping up and to get rid of some of the sap in the grass.'

The minute the match is over, Twynam is down there on his hands and knees inspecting his year's work.

On the day after the champions have all left, when Wimbledon is still a shambles of refuge and human disorder, four male members of the committee step out on to the Centre Court. It was an idea of the chairman, Herman David. He wanted to test for himself if the turf had remained true, if the bounce was accurate. Last year, the immaculate quartet—Sir Denis Truscott, Eric Simond, Dan Maskell and David Mills—had a total age of 251 years.

CHAPTER 24

Strawberries and Cream

To walk round Wimbledon with Sir Norman Joseph is like being with Solomon in all his glory. As head of Town and County, the subsidiary of Lyons, who have done the catering there for the last thirty-seven years, he is a very important person indeed.

Sir Norman lives in that innocuous white tent at the left hand inside the gates. Outside it looks like another piece of canvas, but inside it is replendent like a royal tent in medieval times. The entire walls are pleated with cool white muslin and the cornice outlined in green picot. He has a very small office with sliding glass roof (only a potentate could arrange that in a tent) and the rest is reserved as a large, cool dining area where Sir Norman and guests take luncheon and tea.

It is a very splendid experience to be invited to rub shoulders with past, present and future ambassadors and business tycoons at Sir Norman's table, and the heads of various supermarkets at the other tables. It is all run under the eagle eye of a blonde head-waitress, Miss Nessie Beer. She is a very special person who knows the catering business through and through. Everyone greets Nessie like the old friend that she is, for, along with the tent, she always accompanies Sir Norman to Buckingham Palace, Chelsea, Henley and Ascot. It is in his white sanctuary that Sir Norman, between popping out to see the important matches, controls his empire.

It was in 1936, the great year of Fred Perry and Dorothy Round, that Sir Norman and Co moved into Wimbledon. Now they are the sole caterers for the 30,000 people who attend each day. Most people eat or drink something during the eight hours of tennis each day, and 20,000 meals are served daily.

It is just like a military operation. Ten days before the gates open for play the equipment is moved in. Temporary restaurants and kitchens spring up overnight—2,095 chairs are unloaded, 577 tables assembled, 594ft of buffet and mobile units are erected, 17,000 pieces of silverware, 15,000 pieces of glassware, 15,000 pieces of chinaware and 240,000 containers for drinks have to be sorted out in the various restaurants. There are 60 cash registers alone, and water boilers that can cope with 1,800 gallons at a time.

In the Members' Enclosure—a dizzy oasis of tables with Italian straw umbrellas, pillars twined with roses, icing sugar white garden furniture, great damask-covered buffets in the best Mrs Beeton tradition and a fountain ringed with deep blue hydrangeas -the menu changes every day. The standard is high under the circumstances and the prices comparable with West End ones.

Most people, I noticed, preferred the Vichyssoise to prawn cocktail followed by salmon mayonnaise, half a lobster, salmon mousse, duck and orange salad, avocado pear and prawn salad, and so on. There are dear little Charlotte russes but nearly everyone has strawberries and cream.

At the entrance to the Members' Enclosure for the last thirty-six years has stood Charles Lomas of Town and County, who along with Sir Norman retired last year. Many a domestic crisis has been averted by his skilful juxtaposition of members and their escorts. He knew everyone by sight and name. Wimbledon will not be the same without him.

When Wimbledon opened up after the war, the public's eating habits had changed. They were no longer 'sweet tooths'. Ice-cream sundaes were replaced by strawberries and cream, and today, 1 in every 3 of the 30,000 who attend daily have a portion at 45p a time.

For a fortnight before Wimbledon opened, I followed the strawberry drama because each year has its own problems. I hit last year's wet June. Sir Norman was in daily contact with his catering manager, Louis Avery.

The morning conversation went like this:

'How are they coming on? What is the latest news? Are we getting our daily weather reports? What is the humidity like? What does Covent Garden say? We can't let the public down . . .'

Every morning 2,000lb of strawberries specially picked in Hampshire are brought by van from Covent Garden to Wimbledon. Behind a wall of canvas just to the right inside the gates and behind the giddy little red post office are the sixty strawberry pickers. They are a mixed bag taken from the 100 students, part of the 600 staff that Lyons employ.

It's chilly on that first day as in white coats they sit self-consciously along the narrow trestled tables. Everyone is shy, slow and a little clumsy as they fumble removing the green stalks from the mountains of strawberries. Mrs Parsons, the strawberry mother, bustles among her charges. Several of the boys have ringlets to the shoulders while the girls have tied their shining lank hair into pony tails with odd bits of string. Under the tables, toes wiggle out of sandals. It's comfort at any price.

As one red mountain vanishes another is brought in. There is a crisis. Due to the abnormally wet June the strawberries tend to be large and watery and not too sweet. Someone wants to know from one of the restaurants should there be five large ones to a serving or ten halves. Sir Norman is contacted on his walkie-talkie.

'No half strawberries,' is his edict. So somehow the big and the small have to be juggled. Sir Norman notes to ask Covent Garden for smaller strawberries tomorrow.

The cream is mixed in jugs at the various buffet counters—one measure of single to one of double. This keeps the price down yet gives cream of some substance. Someone remembers that Germans and Scandinavians like to sprinkle castor sugar and black pepper on their strawberries and don't like that blanket of cream. Pepper mills are despatched to the public stands, where the aliens are most likely to gather. The members' restaurant roots for cream and no nonsense.

'What about the Italians?' I interrupted, airing my knowledge gained at Harry's Bar in Venice, 'They prefer fresh orange juice instead of cream.'

This, too, was noted for next year and I wish I hadn't said anything. I can see in darkest January my show-off remark will be discussed at a solemn meeting somewhere in London, for that is how Lyons at Wimbledon try to keep up their standard. Everything must be scrutinised, discussed, accepted or rejected.

Pre-war most of the public went for the 5s lunch, a feast by any standards. Salmon mayonnaise (salmon was 2s 3d a pound then), cold roast chicken with tongue, ham galantine, followed by fresh fruit salad and cream, and gateaux.

With the introduction of self-service, the Wimpy came to Wimbledon. The hours of endless discussion before that fateful decision. A Wimpy war broke out among the committee members of the All England.

The main argument was would Princess Marina, president of the All England, like the fragrance of Wimpies soaring up to the royal box? The Wimpy addicts won and the first bars were opened a few years ago.

The Princess did not like the smell of Wimpies but it was too late. The public loved them. That moment when teeth sink through the slippery onions and first make contact with the knubbly meat before quietly coming to rest on a mattress of bread. Delicious—if you are on the eating end. Today, 45,000 are sold during 'The Fortnight' running neck and neck with 45,000 sandwiches (most of which are now deep-frozen).

In those Wimpy pioneering days, the girls making them had to be paid 10s a day 'dirty money' so that they could get their hair washed daily to take the smell away. Now chefs in white hats do it and accept the smell as part of the job.

In the hot summer of 1971 the Wimpy smell was stronger than ever. Without saying anything to anyone, one of the more enterprising superintendents went out and bought a number of air fresheners which he put under the seats in the royal box one evening. Next morning the plain-clothed security men frisking the royal box nearly had a fit. At first glance they thought they were bombs. There was quite a to-do about that!

Despite the Duchess of Kent's vehement vow that she likes the smell of Wimpies, last year 'Sammy' Sampron, Old Cathusian, member of Lloyds, recommended Lyons to use an 'odour control' machine like the one now installed at his £1,000,000 mushroom farm at Oving, Sussex.

This was done at a cost of £100 a week.

'It's fine when the wind is right but in the wrong direction there is nothing we can do,' says Sir Norman. 'Anyway, the royals don't mind.'

By far the biggest sale, however, goes to the Bath bun, that overrated, smug, sticky little bun that began its life at the royal spa of Bath. It consists of a yeast bun with sultanas, currants and candied peel but the hallmark of a genuine BB is the coarse crushed sugar, called nibs in the trade, sprinkled on the top.

Even the Bath bun has had its own personal trauma. In 1971, a few days before Wimbledon, Sir Norman Joseph was told that the nibs could not be bought.

'What, no nibs for the Wimbledon Bath buns,' he expostulated. 'Impossible.'

With that chummy alacrity that business tycoons have, he called the chairman of Tate and Lyle and Manbre Garton, and explained the problem. Nibs were put into production immediately and the honour of the Wimbledon Bath bun was saved.

Éclairs are very popular with the public (pastries and éclairs 50,000) and very unpopular with the staff because the fondant is always melting. When the temperature soars there is a rush to save the éclairs and put cooling fans over them.

A couple of years ago, Sir Norman sneaked in savoury tarts and these are catching on fast with a sale of 10,000 at 14p and hustling the Scotch eggs, 12,500 at 15p. They may even take over next year, the experts predict.

Mr Avery the catering manager's office is spartan, small and has a deceiving air of confusion. On the walls in front of him are the orders for the day. It's a tricky job that requires he keeps his nerve, and no field commander could do a better job.

With the hourly weather reports coming in he is concerned with the temperature as much as the actual weather. He knows by experience that should the barometer reach over eighty degrees, the demand for food is non-existent and all the public wants is ices, iced coffee, iced lager and soft drinks.

Throughout the afternoon he times his deliveries hourly.

'During a heat-wave three years ago, we were in real trouble,' he tells me. 'A van with over 7,000 cartons of orange drink turned over at Kensington, and we had to send for syrup in bottles and have deliveries by taxis from the various depots. An emergency staff was put to making it up into a soft drink on the site.'

One feels that Louis Avery relishes such crises. His face lights up, his whole being takes on a military stance. It is 'backs to the wall' and all that.

'We've got the strawberry rush down to a fine art. You simply can't over order because of the possibility of waste but on the few occasions when we have been caught out, we send a fleet of taxis all round the nearby suburbs buying up the entire strawberry stock of fruit shops.

'We try never to let the public down.'

Nelson could not have said it better.

During the tournament 195,000 cups of tea and 57,000 cups of coffee are drunk but iced coffee is creeping up at 50,000 glasses. Over 2,000 dozen soft drinks are consumed. Disposable plastic cups may be cheap and efficient, but the public's abuse in throwing them anywhere and not in the many waste baskets, is a sad sight indeed.

Two or three times a day, Sir Norman makes his own regal procession round the fifteen places serving food at Wimbledon. I joined him at 11.30am. It is a stately affair with the sartorially splendid Sir Norman, a small walkie-talkie in his hand, striding out in measured steps. We had a long way to go. We walked slowly, with his eyeballs swivelling round, until they must reach the back of his head.

A skinny young lady stood at the entrance to the strawberries and cream stall. She was smoking a cigarette. Sir Norman sensed that she was a new recruit and stopped her. I could not hear what he said but it was enough that I saw the girl grind out the cigarette between her thumb and first finger.

We pass the public buffets and he asked why the Bath buns do not have butter pats by them. They were, in fact, a few feet away.

'The customer should not have to stretch,' he told the manageress.

In the competitors' restaurant, he asked if the players are satisfied, noting in passing that the fish must have been fried in dirty oil.

'Do they enjoy what we have made or should we make something else?'

Again the manageress reports that the shrimp salad is fine for the players going on at 2pm and the steaks are appreciated by the later players. The fact that the steaks are desperately over-cooked seems to have escaped everyone.

Walkie-talkie calls are made to various members of the staff.

'What has happened to the chairs that should be round the tables in the outside patio in the umpires' restaurant? Is the coffee up to standard?'

Lyons have two men whose sole job it is to test the tea and coffee urns to see that a standard is kept.

We talked about iced lollies, now a great seller.

'Well, there was a little difficulty at first because we had to consult the committee,' Sir Norman told me.

Few of those dear men, of course, had heard of iced lollies. A special consignment was sent to an All England Lawn Tennis and Croquet committee meeting. Solemnly the members—average age over sixty—licked, tasted and swallowed. There was a terrific argument among the twelve men present, until finally it was put

L

to the vote. The decision was then reversed, much to the annoyance of many of the committee.

After the first iced lolly day, the chairman asked for a report on sales. Back came the answer from Mr Arthur Christian, the then catering manager for Town and County:

'Mr David, I regret to tell you that they are going like hot cakes.'

CHAPTER 25

The Girl in the Iron Lung

Miss Margaret Dixon of Pinks Cottage, Selsey, near Chichester, enjoys tennis. She first held a racket when she was two, and used to play at school. She has followed Wimbledon for over twenty years and just like thousands of other fans she has gone there two or three times in 'The Fortnight' for the last fifteen years.

There is only one difference. Margaret Dixon has been in an iron lung for the last twenty-two years.

'It was Harry Hopman, dear friend and captain of the Australian Davis Cup team, who first suggested that I visit Wimbledon in 1955; a somewhat eccentric notion as we lived 300 miles away in Lancashire and I had never been more than 300 yards from my home.

'After a delay of pneumonia and a collapsed lung and various other inconveniences we incredibly arrived two years later at the Centre Court via removal van, guards van, ambulance and the home of previously unknown friends, Professor and Mrs Bernard Neal who live in a house on a hill overlooking the All England Lawn Tennis and Croquet Club. Bernard Neal was croquet champion of the All England Club for four years.

'We had been making plans and detailed lists for six months and friends are always amused by my holiday requirements: waterproofs, umbrellas and parasols seem sensible and understandable, but it is the other impedimenta which perplex them—three different sets of ramps, bowls and buckets and trays for washing my hair and me, and a nursery trolley from which to use them; two bedpans and a bicycle pump; hoists; radio and TV; TV trolley; reading machine (I thought that if I was anticipating time to read it might not rain); typewriter; plugs, cables and tools without which my father cannot move; possum and indicator; positive pressure machine and Ambu (just in case the three other pumps should all fail); fan heater; reading lamp and reading frame; battery charger and clothes horse.'

The journey took six hours in all. In her own method of writing —by breath typing with her mouth—she had written to the All England Club and asked if it was possible for her to come as she would need some facilities. The tickets she could buy herself but not the electricity vital to her iron lung.

And this was done. If you stand on your toes and look just below the royal box on the Centre Court you can see Margaret in her lung edged right up to the court. The lung is placed so that the mirror above her head reflects the area of the court and she can cover it all without moving her head.

Since she moved to Sussex two years ago, Margaret has become a day tripper. But even now it is not a simple operation. Firstly, she is carried in her lung by six sailors from her ambulance, up the staircase and through the passage where the players come at the ground level entrance on to the court. The lung is being kept 'live' with a hand pump. The head of the maintenance department, Mr H. E. Hollis, was called in and a hole was specially knocked in the wall so that once in position the machine can be plugged into the main electricity supply. Then Margaret is set for the day.

She moves into her position some time around 1.30pm just before the royal party arrives and stays there until 6pm, when she reluctantly and tiresomely has to leave "to spend a penny". She does not finally reach Pinks Cottage until 11pm.

Around 4pm, the All England Club sends a silver tray set for tea with Wimbledon éclairs and strawberries and cream.

In 1957 the chairman's wife took Princess Marina down to meet Margaret and talk to her, and in 1969, the new Duchess of Kent who was equally charming and interested. Many of the top players send messages to Margaret. At last year's Wimbledon, Rosa Maria Darmon, the former Mexican player, now married to the former French number one, Pierre Darmon, travelled back with Margaret in her ambulance on the Saturday and stayed two days. They first met in 1957 at Wimbledon and the friendship has developed into something very special.

On that same visit in 1957 when she stayed with the Neals, on the Saturday before the championships began, there was a 'dress rehearsal'. Nothing could be left to chance.

'I experienced the same emotion as I passed through the ivy-covered Centre Court as I had done twelve years earlier, on my first visit, when I literally bumped into Lew Hoad. Everything seemed so unreal and elating.'

All you see of Margaret Dixon in her iron 'home' is her charming face, always smiling, so vital. She has brown curly hair and eloquent eyes that seem to jump about her face, they are so lively. For special outings like Wimbledon, she wears ear-rings. Her neck is padded with cotton wool to save it chafing should there suddenly be a heat-wavy day.

She talks to me in her bewitching voice, rippling with fun.

'I think one of the finest matches I ever saw was when Rod Laver, the right-handed Australian, became champion for the fourth time. The fact that nearly everyone else thinks he is a left-hander is due to their not watching through the mirrors of their iron lungs!

'Isn't this young Chris Evert marvellously disciplined . . . did I see you on television sitting next to Larry King? . . . I do think young Connors put up a good show and wasn't it fun when his mother kept calling "Come on, Jimbo". . . . I hope the sun comes out as I do want to get a tan . . . everyone is so kind.

'Just to be at Wimbledon is fulfilment in itself.'

Another group of people who are entertained by the committee are the 'Not Forgotten' and the 'Lest we Forget' Associations.

This means that daily some thirty permanently disabled ex-servicemen from hospitals all over the country are invited to Wimbledon for the first ten days of the tournament. They have their own seats on the Centre Court and court number 1, and are taken as guests of the committee to the Members' Enclosure for tea. In 'The Fortnight' this means that some 350 disabled see Wimbledon.

CHAPTER 26

Financial Scene

Wimbledon is recognised as one of the world's most exclusive clubs with a waiting list for membership that dates back to before the last war. Only five or six members are allowed to join each year as others drop out, mainly through death.

If you are on the inside—as a member—it means for a nominal sum of under £10 enjoying the most civilised of club amenities, though as a sporting club it is odd that it does not have a swimming pool. It also means that you are sitting on a potential gold mine.

It has been estimated by city financial editors that, in fact, if the All England Club was sold tomorrow lock stock and barrel, the 375 members—300 men and 75 women—would be able to split up the £4,000,000 that their 50 per cent share of the plush 40 acres would fetch on the open market. The Lawn Tennis Association owns the other 50 per cent.

The financing of Wimbledon dates back to an astute bit of thinking by the committee when the club decided to expand in 1922 and move from Worple Road to the present premises. Since then it has regularly issued debentures entitling the holder to a free seat every day of the championship for five years. The current set of 2,100 were issued in August 1970 at £450 apiece and fluctuate upwards on the Stock Market just before 'The Fortnight'. This means in effect that you have paid £10 for a £2 seat but at least you are assured of your place at the Centre Court.

Many debenture holders are large companies who use the seats as business perks in the line of public relations. They rank along with a day out on the moors or salmon fishing in Scotland.

As one advertising company director explained:

'We used to get away with a night at the Playboy Club or Talk of the Town, but now our big foreign clients expect something more exclusive. The wives are content with Sadler's Wells Ballet, but the men want to feel that they are tasting the real Englishman's life and this includes seeing good tennis on the Centre Court. There is simply no use explaining that especially nowadays you can see excellent tennis on the other courts (Stan Smith played on court number 11 last year with only a handful of spectators). Good seats in the Centre Court have more cachet than Ascot or the Derby. It is more exclusive.'

The land and buildings of the club are owned by an entity called The All England Tennis Ground Company founded in 1922, with the shares later divided equally between the club and the LTA. This company is, therefore, responsible for the maintenance of the grounds and upkeep of the entire buildings. The ground company also owns a subsidiary (All England Motor Park) which earns £12,000 a year.

From 'The Fortnight' the All England Club has earned in the past something round £340,000 of which £67,000 came from TV rights, £3,000 from programmes and £270,000 from gate receipts.

From this is extracted the players' much discussed prize money of £50,000 and the annual expenses of running the club. The residue of about £50,000 goes to the Lawn Tennis Association as part of a legal agreement between the All England Club and the LTA concerning the running of the championships during 'The Fortnight'.

The LTA has contracted to play the championships at Wimbledon until 1999. There is a joint organising committee—twelve delegates from the All England and six from the LTA—under the chairmanship of Herman David, who says:

'We all get along with the minimum of friction.'

The LTA assists the All England in the running of the championships. It is a happy arrangement as on top of this the ground company has been advancing money up to the current sum of £300,000 to the LTA which is unlikely to be repaid.

The underlying and important factor in every aspect of the All England Club is that it has always been run by men who know their tennis backwards, who are steeped in the art of playing, in the knowledge of players and in the components that produce great entertainment. The committee especially has always been made up of men who have this tremendous love of Wimbledon.

When I asked the urbane Rex Sterry (son of the great woman player of the 1890s, Mrs Charlotte Sterry) a City solicitor, who is also chairman of the ground company, what would be the attitude to any take-over approach, he answered:

'It depends on the offer. The effect on the committee would be interesting.'

That was as far as we got.

It was the same blank wall I came up against when I asked if there were any women on the committee to discuss the future of Wimbledon.

'Perhaps they don't want to be,' said Tony Cooper, assistant secretary, firmly.

'Ask the men why,' sharply countered Mrs Phoebe Watson Holcroft, a woman stalwart.

But one does get a certain indication that it is possible that parts of the site could be sold off for housing in the future or for a much larger sporting complex built on the lines of those in America with all sports catered for, but the tennis championships taking pride of place.

Meanwhile the All England bathes itself in its succulent green acres and splendid views.

As yet all attempts to collect money from advertising have also been rejected but the winds of change are here.

'I hate to see all this commercialism creeping in,' a member of the committee said to me as we looked at the harmless car full of tennis balls parked outside one of the entrances. The public were asked to guess the number of balls, and the money went to Shelter—a charitable organisation that looks after the homeless. But inside the grounds was blatant advertising.

Every time the cameras show a close-up of a player changing ends, there stands the bottle of Robinson's barley or orange, the label turned neatly to the camera.

Last year, Commercial Union Assurance Company was allowed an advertising scoreboard as a booster for its Grand Prix competition. One presumes that the fact it has contributed £1,000,000 towards prize money for the Master Tournament, under the management of the International Lawn Tennis Federation, makes it sacrosanct.

Despite the fact that there is a large notice in every dressing-room used by the players prohibiting advertising, the blind eye is turned when they all emerge on court with rackets, the strings of which are clearly stamped with a large S (for Slazengers) or D (for Dunlop) that are visible from the top stands.

And whereas Rosie Casals of America last year was chastised at the net by referee Mike Gibson for wearing her American sponsored dress, the national newspaper space she got more than compensated for any inconvenience.

Her argument and that put forward by her lawyer, Larry King, husband of Billie Jean King, was that the dress anyway was basically white and that the enbroidery only occupied 20 per cent of the area. They also mentioned that no one had questioned the British men who blatantly wore the petrol company's initials BP on their shirts.

The best incident happened during a practice game when Kristy Pigeon from Berkeley, California, was asked to cover her faded T shirt bearing the words 'Maharajah Water Skis'. She promptly donned a track suit with the word 'Addidas' (the big United States Sportswear Group) and no one seemed to mind.

The next few years are going to be difficult ones with a piquant situation of Players versus The Committee.

One only had to talk to the women players last year for a few minutes to assess the anger and impatience they have with the partisan thinking of the committee to realise that sparks will ignite within a very short time.

But in a world of mass advertising hysteria, it is also refreshing and audacious of the All England Club who want their women players to remain 'ladies'.

When it comes to world championship tennis they expect men and women of world class to come and give a world class performance. The club provides the best courts in the world, the best facilities for players. To dispense with cunning and garish advertising for 'The Fortnight' seems a very small price.

CHAPTER 27

The Great Australians

To Australian tennis players Wimbledon is the Mecca. It's Home, it's where the 'big stuff' is and it is where they have shone with abrasive toughness since the days of the left-handed champion Norman Brookes in 1914. They have the extrovert temperament, competitive guts, built-in strength, inspirational Harry Hopman and a climate where every child can play tennis the year round.

It has produced a string of names each with a distinctive style yet overall the same hard attacking Big Game—Norman Brookes, Gerald Patterson, Randolph Lycett, Pat O'Hara Wood, J. O. ('Jo') Anderson, Jack Hawkes, Jack Crawford, Adrian Quist, John Bromwich, Frank Sedgman, Ashley Cooper, Lew Hoad, Ken Rosewall, Tony Roche, John Newcombe, Bob Hewitt (who now plays for South Africa), Rod Laver, Joan Hartigan, Margaret Court Smith and Evonne Goolagong.

It was 1905 when Norman Brookes with his sanguine good looks and wavy hair parted in the centre, arrived from Australia as a complete mystery to the Wimbledon scene. He became the first winner of the Renshaw Cup (a memorial trophy founded by the Renshaw family in 1905). His final with A. F. ('The Kiwi Killer') Wilding from New Zealand was the last championship played before the 1914 war when the tournament closed down for four years.

When Jack Crawford won Wimbledon in 1933 no player from

the British Empire had won at Wimbledon since Gerald Patterson in 1922. From the start 'Gentleman Jack' attracted his own following. Quiet and unobtrusive he always played in a long-sleeved cricket shirt with a square-topped racket that gave him a curiously old world look. When pressed hard he slowly rolled up his sleeves and the crowds knew that Jack meant business.

While Tilden and several of the other giants occasionally took a sip of alcohol while changing ends, Jack Crawford had his own tea-tray. It would be set up alongside the umpire's chair—a tray with cup and saucer, teapot, hot water, sugar and milk. Between games he calmly poured himself a cup, drank it and never forgot to fill up the teapot with more hot water for next time.

His court manners were impeccable. Once when playing W. H. ('Bunny') Austin who won the first set against Crawford with a service ace, the crowd heard him call:

'Oh! Well done, "Bunny".'

He was a most generous opponent and never hesitated to praise good play.

Crawford's win over Ellsworth Vines ranks as one of the greatest matches in Wimbledon's history. It was an epic five set struggle with Crawford demonstrating his superb classic style against the American number one seed's intimidating service and attacking powerful volleys.

Mrs Jack Crawford was in the stands watching her husband. Together they had recently won the Australian mixed doubles against Ellsworth Vines and Mrs van Ryn. At the end of the match the strain was so great for her that she promptly fainted from excitement and exhaustion. When she recovered she rushed to embrace her husband through the dressing-room window.

Rod ('The Rocket') Laver, twice champion, was styled 'the greatest player in the world'. The Australians always like a scrap and like Billie Jean King, Laver plays his brilliant best on the Centre Court. He says:

'It's like a surfboard champion riding the crest of a big breaker. When I can no longer play the Centre Court then it's time I gave up tennis.'

In 1970 when Roger Taylor, the tough son of a Sheffield steel-worker, toppled the carroty-headed Australian, Laver said:

'I don't like losing but I have had a good innings. Wimbledon has been a great stepping stone to a lot of things.'

Like most Australians Laver always stays in a flat during 'The Fortnight'. He likes a home atmosphere with his wife Mary who travels with him, and is probably one of the most relaxed and nonchalant players in the business. In the evenings he stays at home looking at Westerns on the television and is one of the few visiting players to Wimbledon who arrives driving his own car instead of using an official car. The Lavers' permanent home is in California.

Ken Rosewall is probably the best player who has never won a Wimbledon title. Called 'Muscles' Rosewall, because you don't notice them, he is an impeccable stroke maker. Bad luck has dogged each of his major matches.

The Lew Hoad family now live on Spain's Costa del Sol where he owns the Campo de Tenis. In a Spanish-style farmhouse set in the foothills of the sierra, Lew Hoad and his tennis-playing wife Jenny are hosts to people who come from all over the world to have tennis coaching and relax in this friendly exported Australian atmosphere.

The Spanish sun has tempered Hoad who once told a Wimbledon umpire, 'Get your ears washed out.' The face that was described as 'hewn from Sydney's Blue Mountains' is burnt dark with a lion's mane of sun-bleached hair. Each year he returns to the scene of his 1956 and '57 victories.

'I'll never miss another Wimbledon,' John Newcombe said last year. As part of the Lamarr Hunt World Championship Tennis Group he was barred from playing in last year's Wimbledon but covered it for the *Evening Standard*.

'Where else in the world are you taken such care of? Those dressing-rooms with their big baths and the masseurs. Nothing will stop me coming back.'

Five months after having a baby, Margaret Court Smith was back in the big time tennis last autumn. Had her timing been

more auspicious, she would have been at Wimbledon. This husky
Australian Amazon, the 1970 ladies' champion, by relentless
training built her body into the most powerful female seen on the
Centre Court since Elizabeth ('Bunny') Ryan. The muscles on
her legs ripple like a man's as she lopes across the court. Off-
setting this she had an agonising fight for years to conquer her
natural nervous temperament.

Her 1970 final was a truly great spectacle as milk-faced with
pain she fought the wily tactics of the mercurial Billie Jean in a
match that lasted 148 minutes with a final score of 14–12, 11–9.

Just forty-eight hours before she had slipped playing Helga
Niessen from Germany and damaged the ligaments in her ankle.
A Harley Street specialist was called in to attend the black and
swollen ankle. She was treated right up to the very moment that
she went on court. The television cameras picked up the pain on
her face as she battled on. Billie Jean has never played a tougher
audience as the Centre Court Crowd willed life into Margaret Court.
When Billie Jean showed signs of cramp the drama was almost
unbearable. After forty-six of the cruellest games that Wimbledon
has ever seen Margaret Court Smith won. Her punishing cross-
court forehand drives had pulled her through.

'I didn't know how long the pain-killing injections would last
but I would have stayed there until I fell over,' she said. And she
meant it.

At Wimbledon she has won the singles in 1963, 1965 and 1970,
the doubles twice and the mixed doubles four times.

The most astonishing of all the unpredictable Australians is
Evonne Goolagong. In 1970 she exploded on the Wimbledon scene
like a breath of clean bush air. 'Instant Spring,' Teddy Tinling
called this daughter of an aboriginal mother and white father.

Infinitely more attractive than her photographs, her pale brown
skin seems to shimmer with an overlay of gold in the sun. Everything is appealing from the tight damp curls on the nape of her
neck to the Mona Lisa smile that flits across her face when she
is pleased with a shot.

In her first year she lost in the second round at Wimbledon but won the plate as a consolation prize. She had tasted some of the glory of winning at Wimbledon and was not depressed.

Back she came in 1971, more confident and as relaxed as a laughing kookaburra. Wimbledon had never seen anyone like her before. She actually hummed to herself as she played her opening rounds and frequently had no idea of the score. She plays tennis as other people breathe and is a natural mover.

The build up to her title-winning match was intriguing. Her two opponents Billie Jean King in the semi-final and Margaret Court Smith in the final expected to pound her with their experience. She had struck a good patch in her tennis. As she waited in the number 1 dressing-room she sang or listened to pop music on her transistor radio. Ten minutes before the forbidding walk out on to the Centre Court, the attendant Mrs Twynam had to put new elastic in her knickers. Evonne hadn't noticed they were sagging and in danger of slipping down.

She went out on to that Centre Court that has petrified hundreds of seasoned players with no inhibitions at all. She might have been playing a practice match back in Sydney. She started like a dream. In the first three games she had a couple of lucky shots. They were better than she had intended them to be. They were more angled than the angle that she was aiming for. There was one shot that she hit down the line that was a winner. It just caught the line. Everything was going for her. Margaret Court Smith found herself playing against some inspired tennis.

It was one of the most wonderful moments for Wimbledon and lawn tennis as you felt 15,000 people solidly behind Evonne. The Centre Court is very fair but they had got completely caught up in this modern fairy tale.

As Dan Maskell says:

'For the first time in my life as a commentator when the cup was presented to her I had a slight tear and felt a catch in my throat.'

This essentially innocent girl took it all in her stride. Never has any champion been so applauded at the Wimbledon Ball where she was escorted by a fellow-countryman Allen Stone.

After the ball was over, Vic Edwards, the man who not only coached her to tennis immortality, but has welcomed her into his family as a daughter, left the hall with his friend Dan Maskell.

Dan turned to him and said:

'Vic, a tremendous performance today which we shall probably never see again. Something to treasure and remember.'

Vic Edwards in his rich warm Australian voice replied:

'You know, Dan, at this hour in the morning we must not get sentimental but it is possible that she will never win it again.'

Some months later when I asked Evonne Goolagong what difference winning Wimbledon made in her life, she said:

'Winning Wimbledon has given me a great honour in life, but it has also placed a responsibility on my shoulders. I have enjoyed the honour and the many pleasures it has brought me, the greatest of which is that I am the first member of my race to win the World Tennis Title.'

Last year, 'Instant Spring' returned, more mature, more serious. She still went shopping in the King's Road for a trendy dress and a silver necklace to wear to the ball, on the day she was to play Billie Jean King. She still had the same private smile but it was obvious from the start that she was not in her best form. When a national newspaper published an artist's impression of her in the nude, she threatened not to go on the Centre Court. She felt so embarrassed.

As she played her important match, I sat with Vic Edwards. She fluffed stroke after stroke. His face remained unfathomable. Only the perceptively quicker puffs on his pipe revealed his feelings.

'She's having another walk about . . . she is as free as a breeze and loose as a goose,' he muttered.

Win or lose, at the house the Edwards family had rented in Chelsea there was a crackerjack Aussie party that night and Evonne never stopped laughing.

M

CHAPTER 28

Kaleidoscope

Each year during 'The Fortnight' brings its own crop of snapshots. The theme is the same but the characters change as new faces appear.

The loving look between last year's champion Stan Smith and his father Kenneth Smith, who was sitting in the competitors' enclosure, when he made his title-winning shot. Mr Smith senior's boyish grin as he reached under his seat and donned a blue paper fun hat that he had brought along just for this moment of family happiness. His parental pride as he shows a bill folder of coloured snapshots of his sons including one of the Wimbledon champion as a babe in the buff.

Nastase flirting madly with the girls in the All England Club's office and warning: 'If you don't give me tickets for my ambassador then I'll have to go to the Russians.' This slender Don Juan easily the most elegantly dressed of all the players in expensive Italian casuals.

Carole Kalogeropoulos, her silken yellow hair falling curtains round her face as she covers coathangers with pink and white braid. Many of the girl players do tapestry between sets. Virginia Wade reads Henry James.

The small Jamaican, eyes like white convolvulus, tucking into the ball boys' lunch of cottage pie, ice-cream and a coke. Recruited from a local school this was his first Wimbledon.

A mountain of rackets collected at night to be taken away to the

Slazengers factory for reconditioning. Many of the players carry their own gut and all are desperately pernickety about the tension. Stan Smith's rackets have a tension of sixty-three pounds and last about six weeks.

In the chintz pink number 1 ladies' dressing-room, trifles and strawberries and cream lined up on the dressing-table among bottles of expensive cosmetics waiting for the players to come off court.

The accurate knowledge that the Americans have of their anatomy. 'I'm creaking like mad,' is how the English girl announces her troubles. 'My deltoid is fine but I've got poor triceps,' says the American. There is a staff of seven physiotherapists provided by the All England Club for the players' use during 'The Fortnight'.

The sight of Mrs Nellie Twynam, ninety pounds of sweet efficiency, counting the laundry at the end of play. One hundred and fifty bath towels of the finest quality are used every day—carnation pink for the women and mint green for the men.

The Centre Court anguish of Larry King, a miniature chess set tucked under his arm to soothe his nerves, as he watches his wife Billie Jean battle for the championship. 'I'll never come here again. I simply can't stand the strain,' he said. Three times a champion, Billie Jean indicates that she will not return to Wimbledon until the women's prize money is increased.

The tears running down Mrs Olmedo's face as she watches her veteran husband Alex Olmedo fighting in the match against the young New Zealander Onny Parun. It had been stopped the day before by rain. He lost.

The Chris Evert entourage. This seventeen-year-old tennis star from California brought to Wimbledon a party consisting of mother, sister and brother-in-law, dressmaker and two priests.

The lady from Blackpool who goes every year to Wimbledon. 'I never see the tennis. I just come for the outing. It is such a lovely place.'

Every year has its incidents. When three demonstrators walked on to the number 2 court in an anti-apartheid demonstration in

1971, the All England Club handled the situation with quiet efficiency.

The chairman, Herman David, immediately reacted:

'I think we must get the umpire down. We must get an account of this. It could be used against Peter Hain who is being very tiresome in his anti-apartheid views. We must have some reliable witnesses.'

In the royal box sat two bishops—Chester and Guildford. Mrs David was sent off to see if they carried a Bible.

Relates Mrs David:

'So I sidled in and sat by the Bishop of Guildford and whispered:

' "Do you possibly have a Bible handy in your pocket?"

'And then I explained why we needed one.

' "Oh, no, but you go and ask Gerald of Chester. He's probably got something," replied the Bishop of Guildford.'

Mrs David then crept along and whispered in the Bishop of Chester's ear.

'Actually I have a New Testament in the car. If you really want one I'll go and fetch it,' he replied.

'Couldn't you swear on Gerald?' inquired the bishop's wife.

Another fascinating incident occurred in 1964. It has only happened once in the history of Wimbledon that a linesman has gone to sleep on the job. It was, in fact, a woman—Mrs Dorothy Cavis Brown.

Hers should have been the voice that cried out when Abe Seigal (South Africa) won match point on the number 3 court and Clark Graebner (USA) sent a ball eighteen inches over the line.

It was such an obvious shot that the players ran to the net.

But there on the backline sat Mrs Cavis Brown, head down, arms folded across her chest, legs crossed, and slumped sideways —fast asleep. It was a Bateman cartoon come to life. The Wimbledon crowd was hysterical with laughter as the umpire sent a ball boy to wake her up.

'I think I became a little dizzy and a little drowsy,' she said, as she left the court.

At noon the Umpires' Association had had their usual cocktail party in the Lodge gardens to which Mrs Cavis Brown, an excellent umpire-lineswoman had been invited. It had been a charming little party, and Mrs Cavis Brown was later to explain to newspaper reporters that she took a spoonful of olive oil to line her stomach before the party and then had one gin, followed by a large lunch.

At a press conference held later, poker-faced, the referee Colonel Legg told a titillated press:

'Mrs Cavis Brown is very tired. She is going to have a rest at home for a couple of days and will not now be on court.'

But, in fact, Mrs Cavis Brown never did return to Wimbledon as a lineswoman. The Umpires' Association held a special meeting and she was barred that year and for evermore.

The only criterion for the Wimbledon Fortnight is the standard of play. There is no racialism or apartheid entering into Wimbledon, and the chairman, Herman David, and committee are determined to keep it that way.

'If they are good enough I don't care whether they are yellow, black, green, Mohammedan, Jew, Catholic or Protestant. I don't care a hang. It is just their standard of play,' he explained.

In 1964 the Russians indicated that they did not want to play against the South Africans. In detail it was a question of Alex Metreveli from Georgia refusing to play Abe Seigal, and Likhachev and Miss A. Dmetrieva not willing to play T. J. Ryan and Miss P. Walkden (who now plays for Rhodesia).

Herman David invited the Russians and two of his executive committee to his office to discuss the situation.

'I had already seen them in Paris and warned them that "if you were going to scratch when you meet a South African, you will never play at Wimbledon. You will not only be stopped at Wimbledon but at pre-Wimbledon activities at Queen's Club.

' "I can't have it and I won't. And with all due respect to your players we shall not miss them much. They are not good enough." '

The Russians went into private discussion before the spokesman replied:

'Oh well, Mr David. I am afraid that you carry too many guns.'

The problem was solved by the Russians giving the South Africans a walk-over.

As committee member Rex Sterry explained:

'The rules are drawn up to encourage friendship between nations in sport and lawn tennis and also to prevent any interference in the game from political influence.'

'I think a lot of people in the world might think we are square,' commented Herman David about the whole affair. 'But we are hanging on to something. It is traditional. It is marvellous and there is something about Wimbledon which we can't ever lose. It is something to do with fairness and keeping up standards.'

The Russians return year after year. As yet they have not produced a champion, but they are there as part of the Wimbledon scene as the New Zealanders, Japanese and negroes.

CHAPTER 29

End of the Story

The winter rain lashed the Centre Court. On this blue-grey day it looked smaller, less frightening, less claustrophobic than in its mid-summer peak. The green paint was blue in the late afternoon light. The shadows in the grandstand were deep and forbidding.

The 10,500 seats had been removed from their permanent concrete bases giving a strange petrified look to this great arena. It was gaunt. There was a feeling of unreality that all this costly construction remains unseen, unused until 'The Fortnight' begins in the last week of June.

I took off my shoes and tiptoed out into the middle of the Centre Court like dozens of players have done before me. The grass was full of sap and squelchy, almost translucent green. Each virgin blade has grown afresh since the championships last year.

Outside the bulldozers were ripping a large ugly hole in the ground to the right of the entrance to the Centre Court. New dressing-rooms on split level for the men players were being built. Every year some of the profits are ploughed back into improving conditions for not only the players but the general public. It is part of the All England policy.

These new dressing-rooms will gain their own character over the years to come. How many famous men players have retreated through sheer exhaustion and disgust at themselves, to weep in the airing-room off the old number 1 dressing-room, to collect themselves before facing the press, their friends, other players and the brutal truth that another year of work faces them?

Television and Eurovision has opened up Wimbledon to a world public. During the first week three to four million see it daily and in the final week the figure leaps to eight or nine million. Wimbledon has also altered the summer schedule of millions of housewives who religiously follow the tournament from start to finish.

The 1920s architecture of the place and the deceptively small area between the edge of the court and the first row of spectators, makes it difficult to place the thirteen cameras. As £250,000 is involved in covering 'The Fortnight' which, excluding the Olympic Games, is the BBC's most ambitious sporting project, A. P. ('Slim') Wilkinson the producer begins his planning as early as January each year.

By June a complete television village has grown up in the adjoining sports grounds. The staff has swollen to 128, about eighty of these being attached to the engineering side. The reporting team is composed of Dan Maskell, the former All England coach, Peter West and Harry Carpenter of the BBC's sports staff and Jack Kramer the former American champion who comes over from California every year.

The mobile staff room with three television sets going buzzes with liveliness at the end of the day. One catches drifts of talk.

'For Chrissake what's happening with that camera . . . where in the hell has Tom gone . . . who's got the schedule for tomorrow . . . tell Jack I want to see him before he goes home . . . make mine a whisky, old boy.'

There is a well set-up interviewing-room and a twee Arcadian outdoor studio complete with white trellis and plastic flowers. Both the BBC sound radio and television have small emergency interviewing-rooms to catch players coming off court. A member of the All England Club's committee must always be present and no player is forced against his or her will. Under these impromptu conditions some of the most poignant interviews have been captured.

Meals are snatched during the day in a jolly alfresco canteen reminiscent of the Battersea Fun Fair. BBC girls, relaxed in trouser outfits and clutching sheaves of papers, dart about like overgrown excited children. There is a wildly undisciplined air about the whole set-up belying its undeniable efficiency. Television cables now run under all the roads inside the club grounds. Colour television presented many problems for covering play as the late afternoon crept into evening but these, too, have all been surmounted by close co-operation between the BBC and the committee of the All England. These tennis lovers, many of whom have been players of considerable strength in the past, are frankly delighted that television has increased the public's interest for tennis.

When the All England installed the electric scoreboards it was the first country to do so. It has since been copied in various parts of the world.

There is a contention among some overseas players that Wimbledon has not progressed the last ten years in the standard of umpiring. There are those who think that with all the money at the All England Club's disposal the fact that Wimbledon has not taken any step towards rectifying blind judging is a let down of a position that they hold as the trustees of a great inheritance. As one such critic said:

'The only thing that one is proud of in post-war happenings is that the All England led the world towards open tennis. But now its concept of tennis management is absolutely stagnant.'

No men did more to pioneer open tennis than the former chairman Sir Louis Greig and the present one, Herman David, a former Davis Cup player. As long ago as 1935 Herman David wrote in *Tennis Illustrated* in an article entitled 'This Wimbledon as I know it':

'Just one subject more, that may have a great effect on future Wimbledons. I believe that open tournaments between professionals and amateurs will definitely come. It may be a good thing. It would certainly clear up many cloudy problems.'

Until some form of electronic control of the lines is perfected there always will be the element of human judgement in the umpiring. The nature of a grass court where a bent blade could throw out the mechanism makes this a difficult one to undertake quite apart from the costs involved.

Every year the club receives many letters from home inventors and fanatics who all claim to have an automatic or electronic answer to the problem. They range from metallic studs on the lines to metallic powder on the ball so that when the metallic ball passes over the metallic line it would produce a bell ringing, to some really outlandish ideas.

Not everyone wants to see these elements of mechanical perfection creeping into the game. As Dan Maskell says:

'Eventually mechanical line calling may come but then you are going to lose one of the whole reasons for playing sport. I feel very strongly about this. When you elect to play sport at school you have a man who is going to officiate. Part of the business of sport is to accept the decision of an umpire. It may have its inefficiencies but this is part of character building, part of life.

'You are robbing sport of one of its great things if you deny men of chivalry and generosity of character the right to accept a decision from a fellow human being. It is only three or four every season who create a fuss. It is remarkable that now when there is big prize money to be won Wimbledon can still discipline the players to accept their judgement.'

Over the entrance arch to the Centre Court under which every player passes is the inscription from Kipling:

'If you can meet with triumph and disaster
And treat those two impostors just the same.'

Every letter of criticism or suggestion for improvement is carefully considered. The Wimbledon fans could be called 'a contented public'. Criticisms from visiting officials are taken seriously. Last year S. C. W. Ackerman, a visiting umpire from New Jersey told me:

'The standard of umpiring at Wimbledon adheres too much to tradition and is not flexible enough.' H. J. Lewis, another American, criticised the calling of the score:

'At Wimbledon the umpire never repeats the "out" or "net"

calls of his linesmen nor do the umpires repeat the scores loud enough. No one questions the decisions but the technique of making the call is inferior and the clarity of the umpire's enunciation is not good enough.'

Much of the success of 'The Fortnight' emanates from the very great regard the All England Club has for its staff and its relationship with them, whether they are permanent or temporary. Everyone has his job to do. From his 'control point', a charming period-furnished office in the main office the quiet introspective secretary, Major David Mills, guides 'The Fortnight' through with the help of his personal assistant Mrs Enid Stopka, an ex-Waaf.

Apart from tennis problems which crop up all the time they cope with the personal side of the players' lives. A car whizzed off to Tooting to hire a dinner jacket for Stan Smith so that he could wear it at the ball last year. Shoes were forgotten so he wore his own brown ones. Arrangements were made for parking the Hewitt's baby in its carry-cot in one of the ladies' dressing-rooms. One year a wedding cake was hurriedly bought and waiting when Lew Hoad and his bride, Jenny, married in the morning, arrived to play. Every year has its favourite whom the crowds take to their hearts. Last year it was the tempestuous and elegant Rumanian Nastase. Long after he had left England the hundreds of letters kept arriving. These were all packaged and sent to his home.

With its own private 'bush telephone' service the committee is kept well informed when disgruntled players huddle in angry protest. The American players' emphasis for bigger and bigger prize money is quietly noted.

The day after the championships end, planning for the next year's championships begins. The office machinery never stops.

Throughout the entire year apart from the club's domestic activities, there are junior, international and Services championships to be arranged and played.

There will always be problems of some sort for the authorities to sort out. Tennis has become big international show business and has created its own stars, jealously guarding their world-wide prestige. But when a player has a Wimbledon title among his references his reputation is secure. This, above all else, is the reason why as long as the All England Club retains its own impeccable standards of quality, fair play and impartiality the future of 'The Fortnight' is secure and why the ticket touts, who have dotted Church Road for the last fifty-one years, will keep on shouting:

'Ten quid for the Centre Court. It's the greatest tennis show on earth.'

INDEX

Page numbers in *italic type* indicate illustrations.